Journal of Biblical Literature
Monograph Series, Volume VIII

THE EXEGETICAL METHOD OF THE GREEK TRANSLATOR OF THE BOOK OF JOB

by

Donald H. Gard, Ph.D.

Assistant Professor of Old Testament
Princeton Theological Seminary

SOCIETY OF BIBLICAL LITERATURE
224 North Fifteenth Street
Philadelphia 2, Pennsylvania
1952

THE EXEGETICAL METHOD OF THE GREEK
TRANSLATOR OF THE BOOK OF JOB

Copyright © 1952 by the Society of Biblical Literature
ISBN 1-58983-230-2

Printed in the United States of America
on acid-free paper

FOREWORD

Dr. Gard's study of the exegetical method of the Greek translator of the Book of Job is a condensation of a larger work on the subject. In its present form it presents what he and the editors believe to be the most convincing examples of the theological tendencies which he finds in the ancient Greek version. It is a pleasant obligation to thank Professor Ronald Williams for his great help in editing the manuscript.

Ralph Marcus
Editor of the Monograph Series

PREFACE

The history of the scholarship on the Book of Job is an extensive
one, as is indicated by representative works cited in the Bibliography. Yet
the author has attempted to present quite a different point of view in this
study.

The writer has examined the contributions which scholars in the
past have made in obtaining an accurate translation of the Masoretic text. A
comparison was furthermore undertaken of the Hebrew text with the Old Greek,
the Targum, and rabbinic exegesis. It is hoped that, as a result of such comparison and criticism, an original contribution has been made for a better understanding of the exegetical method of the Greek translator of Job and incidentally of the other books of the Greek Old Testament.

The author will always be indebted to Professor Henry S. Gehman of
Princeton University and Princeton Theological Seminary for his thoroughgoing
and indispensable supervision of the doctoral thesis of which this monograph is
the result. Professor Philip K. Hitti of Princeton University offered a number
of suggestions concerning style and format for which gratitude is herewith expressed. The author's wife was of much help in checking bibliographical material
as well as in assisting in the compilation of the registry of verses found in
the Appendix. To these individuals the sincere thanks of the writer are due.

Princeton Theological Seminary   DONALD H. GARD
Princeton, New Jersey
September, 1952

TABLE OF CONTENTS

TABLE OF CONTENTS

INTRODUCTION

The writer's interest in the exegetical method of the Greek translator of Job was aroused by Professor Henry S. Gehman of Princeton Theological
Seminary and Princeton University during a seminar course on Job. In this
seminar a comparative treatment of the Septuagint, Vulgate, and Targum[1] with
the Masoretic text showed that in many cases the Greek differed strikingly
from the Hebrew. The Old Latin versions of Job had already been studied by a
former student of Dr. Gehman.[2]

In an article written for the *Journal of Biblical Literature*[3] Dr.
Gehman has discussed some irrefutable examples of the theological approach of
the Greek translator of Job 1-15. As a result of that pioneer work the writer
has undertaken a critical study of the *entire* Book of Job in comparison with
the Greek version. The Vulgate sheds no light on this study. The writer had
hoped that a careful investigation of the Targum on Job would yield material
pertinent to his study. The Targum, however, apparently had nearly the same
Vorlage as the Masoretic text, since it is virtually without deviation from the
Masoretic text.

----

[1]Brian Walton (ed.), *Biblia Polyglotta: Complectentia Textus Originales*
(London: Thomas Roycroft, 1655-1657), 6 Vols.

[2]James H. Gailey, Jr., *Jerome's Latin Version of Job from the Greek
(Chs. 1-26): Its Text, Character, and Provenance* (Princeton: Princeton Seminary
Pamphlet Series, 1946).

[3]H. S. Gehman, 'The Theological Approach of the Greek Translator of
the Book of Job 1-15," *Journal of Biblical Literature*, LXVIII (September, 1949),
231-240.

1

On the basis of Swete's *The Old Testament in Greek*[1] and Rahlf's *Septuaginta*[2] the Old Greek version, hereafter designated as G, has been determined as nearly as possible; in many instances the variants compiled by Holmes and Parsons[3] were consulted as well as the text of Grabe.[4] The Masoretic text used was that of the Leningrad Codex as found in the Kittel *Biblia Hebraica*,[5] hereafter designated as M. All translations from the Hebrew text have been based upon M. In case of difficulties in M reference was made to the variant readings of the Hebrew manuscripts collated by Kennicott[6] and De Rossi.[7]

As a result of the above study, the writer maintains that the Greek translators, who were working probably at Alexandria, used a Hebrew text which is very similar to M. In its translation of the Hebrew text G makes good sense, although its Greek is at times quite Hebraic in its idiom. We may accordingly assume that the scholars in Alexandria had a good knowledge of Hebrew. Their method of translation and exegesis may be discerned by a care-

---

[1]Henry Barclay Swete (ed.), *The Old Testament in Greek according to the Septuagint* (Cambridge: University Press, 1925), 3 Vols.

[2]Alfred Rahlfs (ed.), *Septuaginta* (Stuttgart: Wurttembergische Bibelanstalt, 1942), 2 Vols.

[3]Robertus Holmes and Jacobus Parsons (ed.), *Vetus Testamentum Graecum cum Variis Lectionibus* (Oxford: Clarendon Press, 1798-1827), 4 Vols.

[4]Joannes Ernestus Grabe (ed.), *Septuaginta Interpretum Tomus I-IV* (Oxonii: E theatro Sheldoniano, 1707-1709).

[5]Rudolf Kittel (ed.), *Biblia Hebraica* (3d ed.; Stuttgart: Wurttembergische Bibelanstalt, 1937).

[6]Benjaminus Kennicott (ed.), *Vetus Testamentum Hebraicum cum Variis Lectionibus* (Oxford: Clarendon, 1776-1780), 2 Vols.

[7]Johannis B. de Rossi (ed.), *Variae Lectiones Veteris Testamenti ex Immensa MSS* (Parmae: Ex Regio Typographio, 1784), 4 Vols.

ful examination of G in comparison with M, and this study shows that G did not
set out to rewrite the Hebrew text.   In places where G departs from a literal
rendering of the Hebrew, however, G does follow an exegetical method apparently
in vogue in Jewish circles at Alexandria and no doubt also elsewhere.   This
method by which G produces its renderings of the Hebrew is diversified.   In
cases of departures from a literal rendering which would plainly suggest what
the Hebrew *Vorlage* actually was, the Greek translator may resort to a play on
words or to what Professor Gehman has named a 'trick of the translator'.   The
interchange of ד and ר occurs frequently, as does the substitution of one laryngeal for another.   The expansion of one line in G may also cloak the omission
of another line of the verse in the Hebrew text.   A doublet may be used to
avoid rendering an offensive word or phrase; a change of persons in a verb also
may take place to circumvent some idea in the Hebrew which seemed objectionable
to the translator.   Changes from colourful imagery to matter-of-fact declaration
are often found.   Were there but a few examples of a play on words or of a trick
of translation, the rejoinder may be made that the differences are due only to
style or that they are not based on any particular reason.   The large number of
examples throughout the entire book, however, clearly points to the fact that
a definite exegetical method was followed by the translator.   Furthermore,
the result of this investigation proves that the exegetical method of G has
a *theological* foundation.

   This theological *modus operandi* is quite complex with a variety of
elements constituting the plan.   It is often difficult to establish definite
categories for the different phases of G's exegetical method, because many of
the concepts could be placed under several headings.   The attempt has been made
to place under suitable headings the various types of G's approach to a theological interpretation of the Hebrew, without exercising a mechanical system

of arrangement. The largest sub-division of the group is that which has been
called 'Theological Toning Down' (Chapter I). Here the basis for G's departure
from a literal rendering of the Hebrew text is the tendency of the translator
to avoid ideas concerning God which are abhorrent to him or to his school.
Chapter II (Anti-anthropomorphisms) illustrates G's method of eliminating portrayals of the Deity as having human faculties and emotions. In Chapter III
(Detraction from the Perfect Character of God Avoided) the translator is seen
to subordinate the destructive activities to the constructive work of God.
Originally the writer had included in his study a comparison of the concept of
the future life presented in G with that in the Hebrew text, and examples of
G's exegetical method which do not allow any one general designation but rather
show the trend in G. Since these phases of the translator's method will soon
appear in articles, they have been omitted in this little book. Chapter IV,
'Theological Omissions from the Greek Text', deals with passages omitted from
the Hebrew text by the Greek translator for theological reasons. By a careful
rendering of the verses both preceding and following an omission the translator
attempts to make a logical sequence of thought. Such procedure indicates a
deliberate omission of passages for theological or other reasons. In Chapter V
the results of the study of G's exegetical method are summarized.

Because the material presented in this study is limited to that
which suggests a theological approach by G to translation, it is impossible to
give all the evidence connected with the methodology of translation gathered
in the critical study of the Book of Job. In some passages of the Greek text
of Job there is apparent a certain literary style on the part of the translator,
and at times it may account for the departure from a literal rendering of the
Hebrew text. Such material, which concerns the translator's literary inclina-
tions rather than his theological tendencies, it is hoped will be published at

a later date. In many cases, however, reasons other than literary style must be considered to explain the difference between G and the Hebrew. These reasons are offered in the present investigation.

CHAPTER I

THEOLOGICAL TONING DOWN

This chapter discusses the translator's tendency to tone down passages or expressions in the Hebrew text which do not agree with his view of what should be man's relation with God or his conception of the nature of God. The means by which such tempering of objectionable expressions is accomplished vary all the way from a play on words and a trick of translation to the use of prepositions. The result is an elimination of ideas which are repulsive to the Greek translator. The first theme to be considered, therefore, is the following one:

Ideas Offensive to the Greek Translator

When Job attempts to answer the charges of Bildad, he feels so keenly the agony of his misfortune that in chapter 19[10] he addresses himself to God. This address mounts in vehemence with Job's flinging out an accusation against God (M:10:13):

'Now these thou hast hidden in thine heart;   ואלה צפנת בלבבך
I know that this was with thee.'   ידעתי כי זאת עמך

By 'these' and 'this' Job means evil designs which God has held against him.[1] Even if אלה should refer to the goodness of God which Job has just acknowledged

----

[1]Cf. William A. Irwin, 'Poetic Structure in the Dialogue of Job,' *Journal of Near Eastern Studies*, V (January, 1946), 33-34, for a discussion of אלה as referring to what precedes rather than to that which follows.

as the significant fact in his life, the Greek translator sees the ambiguity involved. He therefore rejects the possible interpretation of the Hebrew that Job could know the heart of God or that God would harbour evil designs against Job. The translator accordingly renders the Hebrew in such a way as to acknowledge the omnipotence of God:[1]

'I know that having all these things in thyself   ταῦτα ἔχων ἐν σεαυτῷ οἶδα
            thou canst do all;   ὅτι πάντα δύνασαι·
There is nothing lacking in power for thee.'   ἀδυνατεῖ δέ σοι οὐθέν.

The third comrade of Job, Sophar, next inveighs against Job with a series of rhetorical questions which culminate in a description of the certain doom of the wicked. Job replies that the lessons of the past must be subjected to discrimination. In chapter 12 he proclaims the mighty activity of God (M 12:16):

'With him is strength and sound counsel;   עִמּוֹ עֹז וְתוּשִׁיָּה
He that erreth and he that leadeth into error are his.'   לוֹ שֹׁגֵג וּמַשְׁגֶּה

The translator, however, objected to the idea of considering one who leads into error as belonging to God. He therefore omits the second line of the Hebrew, expands the first, and renders as follows:

'With him is might and strength;   παρ' αὐτῷ κράτος καὶ ἰσχύς.
He hath understanding and knowledge.'   αὐτῷ ἐπιστήμη καὶ σύνεσις.

Job proceeds with his delineation of the activity of God, but he suggests that God at times acts somewhat capriciously (M 12:20b):

'And (God) taketh away the discretion of the elders.'   וְטַעַם זְקֵנִים יִקָּח

Such an imputation against God is studiously avoided by G, which renders the passage as follows:

'He knew the knowledge of the elders.'   σύνεσιν δὲ πρεσβυτέρων ἔγνω.

After Job has attempted to defend himself before God, Eliphaz and

---

[1]Cf., Gillis Gerleman, *Studies in the Septuagint*, I, *Book of Job* (Lund: C. W. K. Gleerup, 1946), 54.

8

Bildad again upbraid Job. Bildad is especially impatient with Job and gives
a sombre picture of the fate of the wicked. They are to be harassed and tor-
mented while they live. When they die, they are doomed to oblivion. Thus
Bildad portrays the death of the wicked man (M 18:14):

'He is plucked out of his tent wherein he trusteth; יֻנָּתֵק מֵאָהֳלוֹ מִבְטַחוֹ
And he is marched to the king of terrors.' וְתַצְעִדֵהוּ לְמֶלֶךְ בַּלָּהוֹת

The translator did not like this picture of such a violent and rapid removal
of a man by death. He accordingly interprets the indicative as the optative
mood and renders the passage:

'Let healing be violently removed from his abode; ἐκραγείη δὲ ἐκ διαίτης αὐτοῦ
                                                    ἴασις,
Let necessity hold him on a royal charge.' σχοίη δὲ αὐτὸν ἀνάγκη αἰτίᾳ
                                             βασιλικῇ.

Sophar in chapter 20 next shows his lack of sympathy for the plight
of Job. He denounces the wicked, proclaims the brevity of their prosperity,
and affirms their certain punishment. Against this principle of sure punishment of the wicked Job launches an attack in chapter 21. He maintains that
the wicked generally escape their just condemnation on earth. Yet Job affirms
his faith in God as judge. With his friends in mind Job asks (M 21:22a):[1]

'Will any teach God knowledge?' הַלְאֵל יְלַמֶּד־דָּעַת

The answer expected is clearly 'No', but G avoids the boldness of the question
and rephrases the line. The translator introduces his pious observation with
πότερον οὐχί, an interrogative expression which expects the answer 'Yes':

'Is not the Lord he who teaches πότερον οὐχὶ ὁ κύριός ἐστιν ὁ διδάσκων
    insight and understanding?' σύνεσιν καὶ ἐπιστήμην;

God's knowledge is held inviolate in G. Thus it is that when Eliphaz replies
to Job and takes up this statement, applying it to Job, he asks (M 22:2):

'Can a man be profitable unto God? הַלְאֵל יִסְכָּן־גָּבֶר

---

[1]Cf., Robert Gordis, 'Quotations as a Literary Usage in Biblical,

Nay, he that doeth wisely is profitable unto himself.' כי־יסכן עלימו משכיל
Once again the translator objected to the daring of the Hebrew. He avoids the
thought that a man could even be suggested as 'profitable unto God'.[1] He also
avoided the implication of the Hebrew text that a wise man, by virtue of his
wisdom alone, could be of concern to God. G therefore copies its rendering of
21:22a *verbatim* and reads:

'Is not the Lord he who teaches   Πότερον οὐχὶ ὁ κύριός ἐστιν ὁ διδάσκων
   insight and understanding?'   σύνεσιν καὶ ἐπιστήμην;

Eliphaz continues (M 22:4a):

.   'Is it for thy fear (of him) that he reproveth thee?' המיראתך יכיחך
In this passage G may have abhorred the suggestion that Job's fear of God, *i.e.*,
religion (יראה), met with the disapproval of God. The translator therefore construes the Hebrew as follows:

'Or taking thy case, will he   ἢ λόγον σου ποιούμενος ἐλέγξει σε;
   cross-examine thee?'

        In his reply to Eliphaz, Job reflects a changed attitude from his
thought in chapters 9 and 10. There he had argued that even if he could appear
before God, God's capricious might would terrify him into a false admission of
guilt. Here, however, Job feels that, even though God's might still would
terrify him, he could establish his right before God. Thus goes M 23:7:

'There (where Job might find God, cf., vs. 3)   שם ישר נוכח עמו
   would an upright man be arguing with him;
And I should be delivered for ever from my   ואפלטה לנצח משפטי
   judge (God).'

Oriental, and Rabbinic Literature,' *Hebrew Union College Annual*, XXII (1949),
211.

[1]Even if כי be taken as interrogative; משכיל as 'a wise man';
יסכן, as 'be of concern'; and עלימו, as referring to God ('Is a wise man of
concern to him (God)?), one can best understand the difference between G
and M by the method proposed above.

That a man could argue with God or be delivered from him as if from an unjust judge was repulsive to the translator. G affirms Job's confidence in
the justice of God and reads:

'For truth and reproof are from him;   ἀλήθεια γὰρ καὶ ἔλεγχος παρ' αὐτοῦ,
May he bring forth my decision (judgment) ἐξαγάγοι δὲ εἰς τέλος τὸ κρίμα μου.
                at last.'

Job still fears, however, that he will not be able to reach God in order to
be heard by him (M 23:8):

          'Behold, I go forward, but he is not;   הֵן קֶדֶם אֶהֱלֹךְ וְאֵינֶנּוּ
          And backward, but I perceive him not.' וְאָחוֹר וְלֹא־אָבִין לוֹ

To the translator the Hebrew seemed to be an infringement upon the omnipresence
of God. G, therefore, avoids this concept and makes Job confess that he knows
nothing of the last order of things:

'For I go forward, and I am no longer;   εἰς γὰρ πρῶτα πορεύσομαι, καὶ οὐκ ἔτι εἰμί,
And as regards the final things, what   τὰ δὲ ἐπ' ἐσχάτοις, τί οἶδα;
          do I know?'

In this way the translator portrays Job as being humble in his attitude toward
God. In M Job complains because God is not to be found. In G Job merely affirms
his own lack of understanding.

          Job's fear of God in the face of God's omnipotence and omnipresence
is presented quite clearly in the Hebrew. In this same passage which reflects
Job's faith in God and his desire to be heard before God, Job declares (M 23:15b):

          'When I consider, I am afraid of him.'   אֶתְבּוֹנֵן וְאֶפְחַד מִמֶּנּוּ
The idea that Job was in dread of God was offensive to the translator, who accordingly tones the line down and makes Job take admonition from God without
fear:

'Being admonished, I have considered him.' νουθετούμενος δὲ ἐφρόντισα αὐτοῦ.

          In chapter 24 Job takes a broader outlook than that which he had
held in chapter 21. Here he turns his attention not only to the wicked but
also to their victims. He is especially concerned about the fact that God

apparently pays no heed to wrong-doers or to the violence done to those whom
they oppress. Job complains against God (M 24:12):

> 'From the city the dying groan,   מעיר מתים ינאקו
> And the soul of the wounded crieth out for help;   ונפש־חללים תשׁיע
> Yet God regardeth not the folly.'   ואלוה לא־ישׂים תפלה

The translator tones down the last line with its decisive accusation of God.
To prepare for this toning down he employs a trick of translation. In line 1
he substitutes the labial stop ב for the labial מ, reading בתים 'houses' for
מתים 'dying ones' and accordingly rendering οἴκων ἰδίων. In the second line
he substitutes one laryngeal for another, reading חללים 'wounded ones' as
עללים 'children' and interpreting as νηπίων. Line 3 is then changed from the
direct accusation of the Hebrew into a question. As a result the passage is
rendered as follows:

> 'As regards those who were thrown out of   οἱ ἐκ πόλεως καὶ οἴκων ἰδίων
>   the city and their own homes,   ἐξεβάλλοντο,
> The souls of children groaned exceedingly;   ψυχὴ δὲ νηπίων ἐστέναξεν μέγα.
> Why has he not performed oversight of these?'   αὐτὸς δὲ διὰ τί τούτων ἐπισκοπὴν οὐ
>   πεποίηται;

Then Job quotes his friend's arguments in which they have cited examples for the certain punishment of the wicked. Job insists that sometimes
the transgressors are punished, but that such cases are the exceptions which
prove the rule, namely, that workers of violence live to a ripe old age without
receiving the punishment which is their due. In reply Bildad in chapter 25
echoes the words of Eliphaz in chapters 4 and 5. Bildad points out that it is
impossible for a man to be pure before God. To this argument Job in chapter 26
gives an ironic rebuttal. He thanks his comforting friend who has given him
so much help with such gracious wisdom. Then he takes up again his declaration
of the terrible majesty and power of God, until in chapter 27 he reaffirms his
integrity. This time Job uses a solemn oath (M 27:2a):

> 'As God liveth -- he hath taken away my right.'   חי אל הסיר
>   משפטי

Such a statement, however, seems to G to denote an unjust, almost demoniacal
Deity. God has not wronged Job directly. The translator accordingly renders:
'As the Lord liveth, who hath judged me thus.' Zῇ ὁ θεός ὃς οὕτω με κέκρινεν.

In chapter 27 there is a much disputed passage. Verses 7-10 are
attributed to Job in the Hebrew, but the wish is expressed that 'mine enemy'
be as the wicked and that the one who 'riseth up against me' be as the unrighteous. In chapter 21, however, Job had insisted that the wicked prosper and
that the unrighteous receive honour in death. For this reason critical opinion
states two alternative interpretations of the Hebrew: (1) Job has found his
way to a renewed trust in God or has suddenly been filled with the hope of
restoration to God's favour.[1] (2) The reference implied is to Job's *past*
condition, in which Job enjoyed the abundant bestowal of God's friendship upon
him (cf., chap. 29).[2] Driver and Gray interpret the verses as spoken by Sophar,
a suggestion entirely in keeping with the context.[3] The writer, however, holding that these verses were spoken by Job, bases his interpretation of these
verses upon the irony which Job himself employs at the beginning of chapter 26
in his answer to Bildad. Could not Job, embittered and deserted, ask that
his enemy be as the wicked, and his opponent as the unrighteous, in an ironical
sense? This seems to be the best interpretation in light of context, for as-
suming Job as speaker, in the following verse he asks (M 27:8):

'For what is the hope of the godless when   כי מה־תקות חנף כי יבצע
       he makes unlawful gain,

---

[1]Cf., August Dillmann, *Hiob* in *Kurzgefasstes exegetisches Handbuch zum
Alten Testament* (4th ed.; Leipzig: S. Hirzel, 1891), ad loc.

[2]Karl Budde, *Das Buch Hiob*, I, Part II of *Handkommentar zum Alten Testament*, ed. D. W. Nowack (Göttingen: Vandenhoeck and Ruprecht, 1896), ad loc.

[3]S. R. Driver and G. B. Gray, *A Critical and Exegetical Commentary on
the Book of Job* in *The International Critical Commentary* (New York: Charles Scribner's Sons, 1921), I, 226-27.

When God draws out his soul?'   כי ישל אלוה נפשו

Most certainly Job is bitter. His question implies that God does not draw out

the soul of the godless. The translator, however, sets out to make it certain

that the reader will understand that there is no hope for the godless. G also

avoids a false trust in God and asks the rhetorical question:

'For what is the hope of the godless that   καὶ τίς γάρ ἐστιν ἐλπὶς ἀσεβεῖ
    he holds on?   ὅτι ἐπέχει;
Having trusted in the Lord, will he be saved?' πεποιθὼς ἐπὶ κύριον ἄρα σωθήσεται;

In chapter 30 Job sees that his hope for the continuance of his

reputation and state of well-being is now become a mockery. He is bowed down

with the scorn heaped upon him by his former friends and servants. The ravages

of disease grant him no rest by day, no escape by night. Thus it is that Job

addresses his remarks directly to God. He charges God with indifference to his

sufferings and with an active persecution of him (M 30:20-23):

'I cry unto thee, and thou dost not answer me;	אשוע אליך ולא תענני
I stand up, and thou lookest at me.	עמדתי ותתבנן בי
Thou art turned into one that is cruel to me;	תהפך לאכזר לי
With the might of thy hand thou persecutest me.	בעצם ידך תשטמני
Thou liftest me up to the wind;	תשאני אל־רוח
Thou causest me to ride upon it;	תרכבני
And thou dissolvest me into the storm.	ותמגגני תשוה
For I know that thou wilt bring me to death	כי־ידעתי מות תשיבני
And to the house appointed for all living.'	ובית מועד לכל־חי

The meaning of M is that God hides himself from Job's vision at the time when

Job most needs reassurance of his presence. In verse 22 the $K^e\underline{t}\bar{\imath}\underline{b}$ תשוה 'storm'

in light of context is preferred to the $Q^e r\bar{e}'$ה'תשי 'sound counsel'. In ren-

dering the passage the translator apparently chose the lesser of two evils

and believed it less offensive to represent God in his might as persecuting

than as actually causing death to Job. The translator tends to keep God out

of the position of slayer. He therefore omits the second lines of verses 20

and 22 and changes the second line of verse 23:

'For I cried unto thee, and thou didst
    not hear me.
	κέκραγα δὲ πρὸς σὲ καὶ οὐκ ἀκούεις
	    μου,

Thou didst assault me mercilessly;	ἐπέβησαν δέ μοι ἀνελεημόνως,
Thou didst flog me with a mighty hand.	χειρὶ κραταιᾷ με ἐμαστίγωσας;
Thou didst station me in troubles;	ἔταξας δέ με ἐν ὀδύναις,
For I know that death will extinguish me,	οἶδα γὰρ ὅτι θάνατός με ἐκτρίψει·
For earth is a house to every mortal.'	οἰκία γὰρ παντὶ θνητῷ γῆ.

This rendering of G clearly shows that the translator did not attempt a complete rewriting of the Hebrew, but he does deliberately tone down the offensive passages in such a way as to leave traces of the *Vorlage*.

The translation of the Hebrew of the Elihu speeches (chaps. 32-37) shows that the same theological method of interpretation prevailed in this work of another hand as in the other chapters.[1] The Hebrew of M 34:9 goes:

'For he hath said, It profiteth a man nothing	כי־אמר לא יסכן־גבר
That he should be in accord with God.'	ברצתו עם־אלהים

Elihu speaks of Job when he quotes in this verse (cf., 9:22, 28ff.; 10:3).

The translator, however, was loathe to permit any suggestion that there is no profit in pleasing or in being in accord with God, nor did he wish to admit that Job had uttered so sacrilegious a statement. G, therefore, changes' from the third to the second person and from the indicative to the imperative mood of the verb:

'For do not say, There will be no oversight
    of a man,
	μὴ γὰρ εἴπῃς ὅτι Οὐκ ἔσται
	    ἐπισκοπὴ ανδρός·

For there is oversight over him from the Lord.'	καὶ ἐπισκοπὴ αὐτῷ παρὰ Κυρίου.

Elihu next addresses Job himself whom he asks (M 34:17):

'Shall one who hateth right govern?	האף שונא משפט יחבוש
And wilt thou condemn him that is just and mighty?'	ואם־צדיק כביר תרשיע

This is a rhetorical question concerning God who actually does govern and

----

[1]Cf., Driver and Gray, *op. cit.*, I, xl-xlviii; and Paul Dhorme, *Le Livre de Job*, ed. by J. Gabalda (Paris: Librarie Victor Lecoffre, 1926), pp. xliv-xlvi, lxxvii-lxxxvi, for a critical discussion of the Elihu discourse.

secure right for his dominion   The translator avoids the mere suggestion that
God hates right or that man can condemn God, and gives just the opposite meaning
of the first line of the Hebrew by reading:

'Behold thou him who hateth lawlessness   ἴδε σὺ τὸν μισοῦντα ἄνομα καὶ τὸν
Even him who destroyeth the evil ones,   ὀλλύντα τοὺς πονηρούς,
Being eternally just.'   ὄντα αἰώνιον δίκαιον.

In chapter 38 God speaks from the tempest in answer to Job. God
does not lay any charges against Job by attributing to him sins punishable by
the sufferings which Job has endured. Instead, God announces that Job has been
right in maintaining his integrity in the face of opposition from his counsellors.
The comrades of Job had fallen into error by adhering to the contemporary theory
of sin and suffering. They had condemned Job through their own ignorance. Job's
only mistake had been in obscuring the wider purposes of God and in misrepre-
senting the true nature of God. God utters the truth that his range of purpose and action lies beyond all human ability and understanding. This is
brought out by a long series of questions which state the true purposes of God
in afflicting Job. Concerning the laws of heaven God says (M 38:33b):

'Dost thou establish their rule in the earth?' אם־תשׂים משׁטרו בארץ
G eliminates the word 'establish', for the translator implies that no man may
usurp the prerogative of God in establishing the laws of the heavens. Even
though the question in the Hebrew expects the answer 'No', G makes it clear
that man cannot possibly 'establish dominion'; he merely cannot 'understand'.
G, accordingly, tones down by asking a question which expects the answer 'No'.
God asks Job, according to the Greek, whether he can understand:

'Those things happening with one accord   ἢ τὰ ὑπ' οὐρανὸν ὁμοθυμαδὸν
          under   heaven?'   γινόμενα;

Job obviously cannot understand or even know all things which occur with one
accord on earth. The translator, therefore, has succeeded in toning down a

theologically offensive question in the Hebrew.

The translator of the Hebrew *Vorlage*, as the above examples prove, softens ideas which are theologically repulsive to him and to the school of scholars which he represents. He also moderates passages which allow the arrogance of man to appear before God. This introduces the second division of the examples showing a toning down on the part of the Greek translator of the Book of Job:

Arrogance of Man before God Avoided

Chapter 1 shows the assembly of the heavenly host with God and the scene laid for Job's siege of suffering. Only Job himself is not touched by Satan. When the loss of Job's property, family, and possibility of posterity to carry on his name fails to shake his faith in God, Satan gains permission (chap. 2) to touch Job himself. The plot is laid; Job's own physical suffering begins. In utter despair he sits upon the ash heap, scratching his itching sores with bits of potsherd. Then it is that his wife advises him (M 2:9):

'Curse God and die.' ברך אלהים ומת

Such arrogance on the part of Job's wife is avoided by G,[1] which changed the reading:

'But say a certain word in regard to the Lord, (and) die.'	ἀλλὰ εἰπόν τι ῥῆμα εἰς Κύριον, καὶ τελεύτα.

Just what kind of word is to be spoken is not designated -- perhaps one of resignation. At any rate (as in 1:5) G tones down the idea of cursing God.

---

[1]Cf., Gehman, *op. cit.*, p. 237, for a discussion of 1:5; 4:17; pp. 232-34, for a treatment of 9:14-15; 10:2; 13:3, 22.

Job's lack of sympathetic friends, the terrible suddenness of so completely unexpected a reversal of fortune, and his own personal misery -- all these combine to receive outlet in his cursing the day of his birth and the night of his conception (chap. 3). Job, however, does not curse God. He remains true to the Almighty. Such integrity in a man is unknown. Eliphaz (chap. 4) does not even recognize it. He counsels Job with trite phrases and thoughts on the wickedness of man before God (M 4:17). In his self-righteous verbosity Eliphaz tells Job what he would do in such trying circumstances (M 5:8b):

'And unto God would I lay out my cause.'　　ואל־אלהים אשׂים דברתי

The translator sensed the presumptuousness of Eliphaz and therefore renders:

'And I will call upon the Lord, the　　Κύριον δὲ τὸν πάντων δεσπότην
ruler of all things.'　　　　　　　　ἐπικαλέσομαι.

Calling upon God is not so arrogant as laying out one's cause to God, in the sense of demanding something from God.

　　Chapter 9 ends with Job's plea that God take away terror from him so that Job may freely announce his own innocence. Yet, whether or not God does listen to Job's declaration, Job is so depressed that he loathes his own life (chap. 10). From the bitter desperation which is within him, Job cries out (M 10:2):

'I will say unto God, Do not　　אמר אל־אלוה אל־תרשׁיעני
condemn me;
Make me to know why thou dost　　הודיעני על מה־תריבני
contend with me.'

That Job could demand God not to condemn him and to make him know the reason for God's contention with him was too arrogant a concept for the translator. He therefore treats תרשׁיעני 'condemn thou me' in the sense of the root meaning of רשׁע Qal 'be wicked'. The verb הודיעני 'make thou me to know' of the second line of the verse is transferred to the first. In this way the translator

tones down the condemnation and strife of God concerning Job. G reads as
follows:

'And I will say to (the) Lord, Teach   καὶ ἐρῶ πρὸς Κύριον Μή με ἀσεβεῖν
      me not to be wicked,   δίδασκε·
And, Why hast thou judged me thus?'   καὶ διὰ τί με οὕτως ἔκρινας;

In the Hebrew Job had asked for an explanation of his misfortune. In G he

simply asks a question.

        Bildad and Eliphaz again criticize Job for his supposedly self-
righteous attitude toward God. Job in utter dejection feels himself alone
against the entire universe (chap. 19). Sophar offers little comfort to the
stricken man. In chapter 20 he describes the horrible fate of the wicked.
In spite of such lack of sympathy from his human contemporaries, Job maintains
his faith in God as judge (chap. 21). This is construed by Eliphaz as mere
boldness on the part of Job, and so he too takes up the description of the
certain doom of the evil-doers. In chapter 32 Eliphaz speaks of the well-
worn path which the wicked tread. He demands of Job whether he also will follow
the way of destruction, even the way of those (M 22:17a):

        'Who said unto God, Depart from us.' האמרים לאל סור ממנו

The translator removes the impertinence of allowing even the wicked to say to

God סור ממנו and changes the statement to a kind of timorous questioning:

'Those who say, The Lord -- what will he   οἱ λέγοντες Κύριος τί ποιήσει
            do to us?'   ἡμῖν;

Eliphaz advises Job to make his peace with God. He tells Job to look for

guidance from the Lord. If he does so, Eliphaz says to Job (M 22:26b):

'And (thou shalt) lift up thy face to God.' ותשא אל־אלוה פניך

The Hebrew means that Job, through penitent admission of the sins of which

Eliphaz accuses him, will be able to contemplate God. The translator, how-

ever, was offended by such undue familiarity with respect to God and accord-

ingly renders:

'Having looked up into heaven cheerfully.' ἀναβλέψας εἰς τὸν οὐρανὸν ἱλαρῶς·
In this way the Greek translator has been consistent with the concept that no
man can see God and live (cf., Exod. 33:20).

In the chapters 23 and 24 Job's broader outlook on his own suffering does not prevent him from seeking out the reason for it all from God.
Bildad merely repeats the platitudes of his friends, offering meagre comfort
to Job in chapter 25. Job, however, continues to maintain his initial declaration that he has committed no sin of such grave import as to deserve his present affliction. In chapter 27 Job ironically says that the hope of the godless disappears when God demands his soul. Thus it is that in his closing
monologue (chaps. 29-31) Job reviews his own past life and present condition.
He tries in vain to understand why it is that God should cause him so much
suffering in spite of his blameless life. In denying the many sins which he
lists in chapter 31, Job points out that he has always been just in his treatment of his servants. He explains that if he had not been fair in his dealings, he would not be able to do anything when God appears to him for reckoning. Job says (M 31:14b):

'And when he (God) visits, what shall I answer him?' וכי־יפקד מה אשיבנו
The translator avoids the idea of answering God directly by omitting the in-
direct object. G reads:

'And if (he makes) a visitation, what ἐὰν δὲ καὶ ἐπισκοπήν, τίνα
answer shall I make?' ἀπόκρισιν ποιήσομαι;

In the Hebrew of M 31:33-40 there is a problem of a textual nature
which may not be evaded. Verses 33, 34, and 38-40 present a detailed list of
sins which Job has avoided. Verses 35-37, however, record Job's passionate
assertion that he is ready to have his entire life laid bare before God. Job
is convinced that he will be brought into the presence of God. Because of this
difference in subject matter, many scholars have insisted that verses 35-37

are misplaced. Opinion is divided, however, on the original position of these verses. Cheyne places them at the beginning of chapter 31.[1] Driver and Gray (following Delitzsch, Budde, Hontheim, Merx, and Duhm) maintain that verses 38-40b are the ones which have been misplaced, and that the original position of verses 38-40b was somewhere between verse 5 and verse 35. In translating the Hebrew Driver and Gray place verses 38-40 after verse 34.[2]

It is the opinion of this writer that originally M 31:38-40 followed directly after M 31:34. As will be seen in the detailed discussion of this passage (M 31:33-40) the original ending would have been what is now M 31:37 -- a strong statement by Job of his defiance of God. Such an attitude on the part of the hero of the story was avoided by the Sōp^erîm. They therefore placed what is now M 31:38-40 in its present position. This change must have taken place before the work of the Septuagint translators. The present order of M was in the *Vorlage* of G, for G has the same order of verses as M. In his discussion of these verses, therefore, the writer considers the sequence of M.

In M 31:33-40 Job delivers a long recitation of hypothetical sins. Because he maintains that he is innocent of such transgressions, he introduces them by a series of conditional clauses. The apodosis is found in M 31:40. Job declares (M 31:33-34):

'If after the manner of man I concealed my transgressions,   אם־כסיתי כאדם פשעי
By hiding mine iniquity in my bosom --   לטמון בחבי עוני
Because I feared the great multitude,   כי אערוץ המון רבה
And the contempt of the clans terrified me,   ובוז־משפחות יחתני
So that I kept silence and went not out of the door,'   ואדם לא־אצא פתח

The Hebrew presents Job as committing transgression of his own accord, so that

---

[1] T. K. Cheyne, 'Job (Book),' *Encyclopaedia Biblica*, ed. by T. K. Cheyne and J. S. Black (New York: The Macmillan Co., 1899-1903), II, 2479.

[2] Driver and Gray, *op. cit.*, I, 261-62.

he feared the censure of the populace. In G, however, verse 33 is contracted,

and the addition of the adverb ἀκουσίως portrays Job as an unwilling transgress-

or. Even though M portrays Job as fearful of the clans, the Greek translator

may very well have seen the theological implication that Job fears men rather

than God. This kind of arrogance before God is avoided in G. The translator

further enhances the character of Job in verse 34 by depicting Job as an

honest man, unafraid to acknowledge his sin in the face of the people. G reads

as follows:

'If, however, having sinned unwillingly, I hid my sin; --	εἰ δὲ καὶ ἁμαρτὼν ἀκουσίως ἔκρυψα τὴν ἁμαρτίαν μου,
For I was not overawed by the great crowd of the multitude (so as) not to declare it before them --	οὐ γὰρ διετράπην πολυοχλίαν πλήθους τοῦ μὴ ἐξαγορεῦσαι ἐνώπιον αὐτῶν·
And if I allowed a poor man to go out my gate with empty bosom:'	εἰ δὲ καὶ εἴασα ἀδύνατον ἐξελθεῖν θύραν μου κόλπῳ κενῷ·

The translator added the further commending feature to the character of Job

by supplying the line which tells of Job's charity toward the poor. The

Hebrew of the following verses presents Job's defiant cry (M 31:35-37):

'Oh that I had one to hear me!	מי יתן־לי שמע לי
Behold, here is my Taw (i. e., mark): let the Almighty answer me!	הן תוי שדי יענני
And the indictment which mine adversary wrote	וספר כתב איש ריבי
Surely upon my shoulder would I carry it,	אם־לא על־שכמי אשאנו
I would bind it around me as a crown;	אענדנו עטרות לי
I would declare unto him the number of my steps,	מספר צעדי אגידנו
As a prince would I go near unto him.'	כמו־נגיד אקרבנו

The thought of verse 35 in the Hebrew was objectionable to the translator for three

reasons: (1) It implies that God does not hear man. (2) It is impertinent of

Job to demand that the Almighty answer him. (3) It is abhorrent to the trans-

lator to consider God as an adversary who writes out an indictment against Job.

G eliminates the first difficulty by omitting the first line of the verse. It

then resumes the sequence in Greek of the conditional clauses, for the render-

ing of the second line. In the third line the translator overruled the objection-

able feature by having Job presented as the owner of an agreement (συγγραφή)

between himself and someone probably indebted to him. The arrogance of Job's
likening himself to a prince who would declare things to God and would come
up before him is eliminated by G's rendering of verse 37. G had made good sequence with the use of εἰ clauses, and considers the συγγραφή as one between
Job and another human, instead of the Hebrew's concept of an indictment from
God. The translator accordingly renders the Hebrew:

'And if I had not feared the hand of the Lord;--	χεῖρα δὲ Κυρίου εἰ μὴ ἐδεδοίκειν,
But as for the writing which I had concerning anyone	συγγραφὴν δὲ ἣν εἶχον κατά τινος
Having placed it about (my) shoulders as a garland, I acknowledged it +-	Ἐπ' ὤμοις ἂν περιθέμενος στέφανον ἀνεγίνωσκον,
And if, having broken it, I had not made it good; --	καὶ εἰ μὴ ῥήξας αὐτὴν ἀπέδωκα,
Taking nothing from a debtor --'	οὐθὲν λαβὼν παρὰ χρεωφιλέτου·

In this manner the translator avoids the arrogance attributed to Job and portrays him as a man who keeps his word.

The Hebrew resumes the protases of Job's defence of himself in M
31:38-39:[1]

'If my land has cried out against me,	אם־עלי אדמתי תזעק
And the furrows thereof wept together;	ויחד תלמיה יבכיון
If I have eaten its produce without paying,	אם־כחה אכלתי בלי־כסף
And caused the owners thereof to expire;'	ונפש בעליה הפחתי

The Hebrew uses the expression כחה 'its strength' (M 31:39a) to denote the
produce of the field. The translator renders literally τὴν ἰσχὺν αὐτῆς to
denote the same concept. The Hebrew בלי־כסף is rendered in the same line as
ἄνευ τιμῆς 'without price, compensation', an interpretation which carries the
same connotation as the Hebrew 'without money', i. e., without paying. The
second line of M 31:39 has the expression בעליה 'lords, owners thereof'.
Although the word is plural in number, the translator avoids it because of

----

[1]Although 31:38-39 is not an example of the translator's avoiding the arrogance of man before God, it is discussed here to illustrate the
translator's method of interpreting the entire passage 31:33-40b.

its suggestion of the heathen $B^{e'}\bar{a}l\bar{\imath}m$. The translator therefore adds ψυχή

'desire, will',[1] and renders as follows:

'If my land ever cried out against me; εἰ ἐπ' ἐμοί ποτε ἡ γῆ ἐστέναξεν,
And if the furrows thereof wept together;εἰ δὲ καὶ οἱ αὔλακες αὐτῆς ἔκλαυσαν ὀμουμαδόν·
And if I alone have eaten the strength thereof εἰ δὲ καὶ τὴν ἰσχὺν αὐτῆς ἔφαγον
   (i. e., the produce thereof) without compensation; μόνος ἄνευ τιμῆς,
And if I caused distress, rejecting the will εἰ δὲ καὶ ψυχὴν κυρίου τῆς γῆς
   of the lord of the land;' ἐκλαβὼν ἐλύπησα·

Now Job comes to the apodosis of his declamation. He feels himself so free of

the sins which he has listed in the conditional clauses that he concludes his

monologue by calling dire misfortune upon himself if he has transgressed (M 31:40ab):

'Instead of wheat let thorns come forth; תחת חטה יצא חוח
And instead of barley, noxious weeds.' ותחת־שערה באשה

G makes a good translation:

'Then in place of wheat may there come up nettles;ἀντὶ πυροῦ ἄρα ἐξέλθοι μοι κνίδη,
And in place of barley, brambles.' ἀντὶ δὲ κριθῆς βάτος.

   Elihu takes the floor now and proceeds to summarize the arguments

which Eliphaz, Bildad, and Sophar had already advanced against Job. He also

accuses Job of self-righteousness before God (M 35:2):

'Dost thou consider this as right, הזאת חשבת למשפט
(That) thou sayest, 'My righteousness אמרת צדקי מאל
   before God?'

The translator retains the meaning of the Hebrew, even though he usually avoids

having any expression which denotes arrogance before God. For this reason the

translator allows the verse to stand but adds the expressions τί 'what?' and

σὺ τίς εἶ 'who art thou?' to tone down the abruptnees of the Hebrew. G ac-

cordingly reads:

'What is this that thou dost consider as right? Τί τοῦτο ἡγήσω ἐν κρίσει;

-----

[1]Cf. J. F. Schleusner, *Novus Thesaurus philologico-criticus sive lexicon in LXX et Reliquous Interpretes Graecos ac scriptores apocryphos Veteris Testamenti* (Leipsig: In Libraria Weidmannia, 1820-1821), *sub voce*.

Who art thou that thou shouldst say,   σὺ τίς εἶ ὅτι εἶπας Δίκαιός εἰμι
    I am just before God?'   ἔναντι Κυρίου;

      Because he has spoken for so long a time without interruption,

Elihu in chapter 36 tries to justify the continuance of his speaking. He

says (M 36:2):

    'Suffer me a little, and I will tell thee; כַּתַּר־לִי זְעֵיר וַאֲחַוֶּךָ
    For there are yet words on God's behalf.' כִּי עוֹד לֶאֱלוֹהַּ מִלִּים

The second line of the Hebrew is especially offensive to the translator. To

say that there is still something to be said for God was too impertinent a

statement. G accordingly tones down and renders the Hebrew as follows:

'Wait for me yet a little that I may   Μεῖνόν με μικρὸν ἔτι ἵνα διδάξω σε·
      teach thee;
For there is still speech within me.'   ἔτι γὰρ ἐν ἐμοί ἐστιν λέξις.

      Elihu finishes his speech at the end of chapter 37. God himself

now begins his reply to Job in chapter 38. After asking Job to consider the

mighty works of creation and of the regulation of the universe he demands of

Job (M 40:8):

    'Wilt thou even frustrate my judgment?   הַאַף תָּפֵר מִשְׁפָּטִי
    Wilt thou condemn me that thou mayest be justified?' תַּרְשִׁיעֵנִי לְמַעַן תִּצְדָּק

Even though God speaks, the translator avoids the suggestion of having Job

accused of frustrating God's judgment or of condemning him. The first line

is toned down by changing from a question to a command. The blasphemy of

the second line is eliminated by rendering so as to show the purpose of God's

treatment of Job:

'Do not set aside my judgment!   μὴ ἀποποιοῦ μου τὸ κρίμα.
But dost thou think I have dealt with thee οἴει δέ με ἄλλως σοι κεχρηματικέναι
    otherwise than in order that thou mayest   ἢ ἵνα ἀναφανῇς δίκαιος;
    plainly appear righteous?'

      In other words the translator of the Book of Job has followed an

exegetical method which not only softens ideas offensive to him but also tones

down or eliminates the arrogance of man in the presence of God.

Removal of the Name of God When Its Retention Would

Detract from the Perfect Character of God

In the Hebrew of the Book of Job the sufferings and loneliness
which Job endures are accepted by Job with mixed feelings. Job maintains that
he is innocent of any disobedience to God. He cannot therefore, understand
why it is that God as the omnipotent Lord of the universe would bring such
affliction upon him. As any man reacts to real or imagined injustice, so
Job vacillates in his attitudes toward his friends from that of condemnation
to that of irony. At times he pleads for the friendship of God and at other
times speaks of God as being demoniacal and capricious.

The translator, however, is well-disposed to Job, always attempting to portray him as one who submits to discipline from God with patience.
Whenever possible, G removes any abhorrent or offensive idea by employing the
methods seen in the first two divisions of this chapter. At times, however,
the translator removes the name of God from a passage to avoid attributing to
Job any derogatory concept of the character of God.

In his reply to the first speech of Sophar Job decries the extremity
of his position. He says (M 12:4):

'I am to be (as one who is) a laughing-stock to his neighbour, שְׂחֹק לְרֵעֵהוּ אֶהְיֶה
One who calls upon God, and he answered him. קֹרֵא לֶאֱלוֹהַּ וַיַּעֲנֵהוּ
A laughing-stock is the just, the perfect man.' שְׂחוֹק צַדִּיק תָּמִים

The translator omits the first two lines of the verse for one of two reasons:
(1) In M 9:16 Job had complained that God did not answer his cry. (2) Line
1 of this verse begins with the same word as does line 3, namely, שְׂחֹק 'laughing-stock'; homoeoarchy, however, could have caused the omission of the inter-
vening lines. At any rate G keeps God out of Job's statement, thereby avoiding
any idea of injustice as regards the dealings of God with man. G therefore

renders only line 3. The translation is as follows:

'For the just man and blameless has become δίκαιος γὰρ ἀνὴρ καὶ ἄμεμπτος
     mockery.'   ἐγενήθη εἰς χλεύασμα·

Sophar hears such words with impatience. He replies (chap. 20) to Job's discourse by insisting that the wicked never prosper for long. He depicts the greed with which evil-doers gorge themselves upon ill-gotten wealth but adds the rather coarse observation that they must vomit up their riches. Sophar says concerning the riches of the wicked (M 20:15b):

'Out of his (the wicked's) belly God doth cast them (up).' מבטנו יורשנו אל

The translator wishes to avoid the crude figure of God's casting ill-gotten wealth from a man's belly, and so omits the name of God by rendering אל as ἄγγελος 'an angel'. He then plays with בטן, reading it as בית 'house'. G accordingly renders:

'Out of his house an angel will drag   ἐξ οἰκίας αὐτοῦ ἐξελκύσει
    it (ill-gotten wealth).'   αὐτὸν ἄγγελος.

As Job takes up his final discourse (chap. 29), he longs for the former days before his trials began. He wishes that he were as at that time (M 29:5a):

'When the Almighty was yet with me.' בעוד שדי עמדי

The translator objects to the idea that God has deserted Job. He therefore plays with the words בעוד שדי. He treats the labial ב as מ, yielding the adverb מעוד 'exceedingly'. In שדי he treats ד as י, yielding the noun שדי 'field'. He then translates מעוד שדי as ὑλώδης λίαν 'exceedingly wooded' and renders the verse as follows:

'When I was exceedingly wooded.'   ὅτε ἤμην ὑλώδης λίαν.

The meaning which the translator thus obtains is that Job in his former prosperity enjoyed the ownership of extensive uncultivated or pasture lands -- a certain sign of wealth in an arid country. In other words Job does not charge

God with having deserted him.

The passages treated above illustrate the method of the translator in removing the name of God from his rendering of the Hebrew text whenever the retention of the name would detract from the perfect character of God.

Use of Prepositions to Tone Down Ideas Offensive

to the Greek Translator

In the prose section which comprises the prologue to the Hebrew Book of Job (chaps. 1-2) Satan is represented as coming with the בני אלהים 'sons of God' before God. The Hebrew of M 1:6 reads that they came:

'. . . to present themselves before Yahweh.' להתיצב על־יהוה

The preposition על 'upon, over, before' usually is rendered by the Greek as ἐπί 'upon, against' or ὑπέρ 'over, above'. The translator, however, makes certain that the passage will be interpreted as meaning that the בני אלהים stand *before* Yahweh, not *against, above* him. G therefore employs the preposition ἐνώπιον 'before the face of, in the presence of' and renders:

'. . . to come forward before the face of παραστῆναι ἐνώπιον τοῦ κυρίου. the Lord.'

In the first exchange of words between Satan and the Lord the Hebrew reads (M 1:9):

'Then the Satan answered Yahweh.' ויען השטן את־יהוה

The translator objected to Satan's answering the Lord directly. Accordingly he employs the preposition ἐναντίον 'in the presence of' and renders the Hebrew as follows:

'Then the Devil answered and said in the ἀπεκρίθη δὲ ὁ διάβολος κc᾽ εἶπεν presence of the Lord.' ἐναντίον τοῦ κυρίου.

This tendency is not, however, universally carried out. In M 1:7 the Hebrew goes:

'And the Satan answered Yahweh.' ויען השׂטן את־יהוה

Here the translator renders literally. In the second discussion of Satan with God, however, the translator again tones down the Hebrew by use of a preposition. M 2:2 reads:

'And the Satan answered Yahweh.' ויען השׂטן את־יהוה

As in 1:9 G renders:[1]

'Then the Devil spoke before the face of   τότε εἶπεν ὁ διάβολος ἐνώπιον
      the Lord.'   τοῦ κυρίου.

As the sons of God assemble a second time (chap. 2), Satan again joins himself to the group. The Hebrew of M 2:1 reads:

'And the Satan also came in their midst to   ויבוא גם־השׂטן בתכם
      present himself to Yahweh.'   להתיצב על־יהוה

The translator, as in 1:6, objects to the use of the preposition על in this connection. He therefore omits the words להתיצב על־יהוה. Thus Satan does not present himself to God; he merely is in the midst of the בני אלהים. G reads: 'And the Devil also came in their midst.' καὶ ὁ διάβολος ἦλθεν ἐν μέσῳ αὐτῶν. Origen, however, inserts the rest of the Hebrew under the asterisk, thus showing that it was not represented in the Old Greek.

After all the misfortune has come upon him, Job hears his wife advise him to curse God and die. Yet Job rebukes her and retains his faith in God. Thus it is that the Hebrew reads concerning Job (M 2:10):

'. . . Job did not sin with his lips.' לא־חטא איוב בשׂפתיו

The translator felt that there could be the possibility of Job's having sinned inwardly in his thoughts. He therefore eliminates such a possibility by adding the phrase ἐναντίον τοῦ θεοῦ 'in the presence of God' to show that Job's integrity is without blemish and that sin is an offence before God. G therefore

----

[1]Cf., Gehman, *op. cit.*, p. 239, for a discussion of 1:9 in this connection.

reads:

'. . . Job did not sin with his lips in οὐδὲν ἥμαρτεν Ἰὼβ τοῖς χείλεσιν
the presence of God.' ἐναντίον τοῦ θεοῦ.

In the self-righteous counsel which Bildad gives Job in chapter 8 Bildad implies that Job's children have been slain because of their own transgressions (M 8:4a):

'If thy children have sinned against him.' אם־בניך חטאו־לו

The translator recognizes that sin is an offence against God. A man does, however, sin in the presence of God. For these reasons G employs the preposition ἐναντίον 'before' and renders:

'If thy children have sinned in εἰ οἱ υἱοί σου ἥμαρτον
his presence.' ἐναντίον αὐτοῦ.

In his reply to Bildad Job acknowledges that no one is perfect before God (chap. 9). He asks (M 9:2b):

'And how can a man be just with God?' ומה־יצדק אנוש עם־אל

Gesenius-Buhl renders עם־אל. . . צדק in this verse as *Gerecht sein (d. i., nach Gottes Sinn.*[1] Wolff, however, treats it as *'gegen, im Vergleiche zu, wie ar.* ع'.[2] The translator removes the ambiguity by using the preposition παρά 'before,with, beside' and renders the verse:

'For how will a mortal be just before πῶς γὰρ ἔσται δίκαιος βροτὸς παρὰ
the Lord?'[3] Κυρίῳ;

Eliphaz feels called upon to defend the traditional point of

---

[1]Wilhelm Gesenius, *Hebräisches und Aramäisches Handwörterbuch über das Alte Testament,* ed. Frants Buhl (Unveränderter Neudruck der 1915. erschienen 17. Auflage: Göttingen: Springer Verlag, 1949).

[2]M. Wolff, 'Analekten,' *Zeitschrift der Deutschen Morgenlandischen Gesellschaft,* LIV (1900), 8-16.

[3]Elihu repeats this same question in M 25:4a: 'How then can a man be just with God?' ומה־יצדק אנוש עם־אל. G again objects to the use of the preposition עם, rendering it as παρά 'before': 'For how will a mortal be just before the Lord?'

view on suffering, namely, that suffering is the direct result of sin. He
shows to his own satisfaction in chapter 15 that in reality the wicked are
punished. He says that their lot is mental anguish and terror. When Job replies to Eliphaz, it is to plead for an intercessor who would be witness before
God as to his innocence. Job asks for such an one for the following reason
(M 16:21a):

'That he would decide for a man with God.' ויוכח לנבר עם־אלוה
The translator objects to the idea of conflict with God which could be interpreted from the use of the preposition עם. G employs the preposition
ἔναντι 'before' and renders:
'Let there be refutation to a man before God.' εἴη δὲ ἔλεγχος ἀνδρὶ ἔναντι Κυρίου.

In the Elihu discourse (chaps. 32-37) Job's complaint that God does
not answer or speak to him is taken up. Elihu maintains that God has actually
spoken through dreams and visions and that Job merely has failed to hear God.
He accuses Job of speaking without knowledge or discretion. He cries (M 34:
36-37):

'Would that Job were tried unto the end	אבי יבחן איוב עד־נצח
Because of his answering like wicked men;	על־תשבת באנשי־און
For he addeth unto his sin rebellion;	כי יסיף על־חטאתו פשע
Among us he clappeth (his hands)	בינינו יספוק
And multiplieth his words against God.'	וירב אמריו לאל

The translator, however, sees in Job an innocent man. He therefore interprets the Hebrew of verse 36 so that Elihu admonishes Job to gain understanding. By changing from the third person singular to the first person plural in
line 1 of verse 37, by omitting the word פשע, and by adding the negative μή,
G includes all men as sinners. The translator next removes the contempt which
Job exhibits in the Hebrew of line 2 and charges all men with lawlessness.
That any man could multiply words against God is toned down by the use of the
preposition ἐναντίον 'before' for the Hebrew ל in לאל 'against God' of line 3.

G has, therefore, made a pious change in these verses. In the Hebrew Elihu

accuses Job; in the Greek, all men. In the Hebrew Job alone has sinned;

in the Greek, all men. The Hebrew is particular in application; the Greek,

universal G reads as follows:

'But nevertheless learn, Job!	οὐ μὴν δὲ ἀλλὰ μάθε, 'Ιώβ,
Do not again answer as (do) foolish men	μὴ δῷς ἔτι ἀνταπόκρισιν ὥσπερ οἱ ἄφρονες
So that we will not add to our sins;	ἵνα μὴ προσθῶμεν ἐφ' ἀμαρτίας ἡμῶν,
But lawlessness will be spoken against us,	ἀνομία δὲ ἐφ' ἡμῖν λογισθήσεται,
Having spoken many words before the Lord.	'πολλὰ λαλούντων ῥήματα ἐναντίον τοῦ κυρίου.

The examples cited in this chapter on the exegetical method of the

Greek translator of the Book of Job prove that there is more than haphazard style

behind the departures from a literal rendering of the Hebrew. There is a defi-

nite tendency on the part of G to tone down ideas which were offensive to him,

to remove the name of God from a passage when its retention would detract from

the perfect character of God, and finally to employ prepositions which remove

ideas at variance with the theology prevailing in Hellenistic-Jewish circles.

The basis of such toning down is to be found in a theological approach to

exegesis.

CHAPTER II

ANTI-ANTHROPOMORPHISMS

That the Greek translator of the Book of Job followed an exegetical method based on theological considerations has been discussed in Chapter I. In addition to following a policy of toning down certain passages of the Hebrew, the translator also avoided certain anthropomorphic expressions concerning God. This procedure on the part of the translator is but one part of the total exegetical method of the Greek translator. The use of anti-anthropomorphisms is not the main purpose of the Greek translator, but it does serve to show one essential phase of the hermeneutical method employed in G.[1]

This chapter, therefore, deals with the removal by the translator of any portrayal of God in human form. As the first subdivision of this topic there should be considered the following:

The Removal of References to Parts of the

Human Body or their Functions

In chapters 23 and 24 Job states the dilemma with which he is confronted. He asks why it is that so often the victims of wickedness suffer without God's taking note of the wicked themselves. He says of God (M 24:23):

'He granteth him (the wicked) to be confident,   יתן־לו לבטח
    and he stands supported;   וישען

----

[1]The writer agrees with the statement of Gehman, op. cit., p. 237: 'It can hardly be assumed that he [the Greek translator] deliberately set out to remove anthropomorphisms. In view of the theological coloring of G, the anti-anthropomorphisms are only a part of the exegetical pattern.' Cf. Gehman, ibid., for a discussion of 10:4, 14:3a, 15:15, where G makes use of anti-anthropomorphisms.

32

'And his eyes are upon their ways.' ועיניהו על־דרכיהם

The translator objects to the idea in line 1 that God supports an oppressor.
He further objected to the use of 'his eyes' as referring to God in an anthropomorphic sense of sight. The translator therefore changes the thought of the
lines to show that there is retribution for the wicked. The translator then
omits עיניהו and renders as follows:

'Having become weak, let him not hope to be-   μαλακισθεὶς μὴ ἐλπιζέτω ὑγιασ-
   come healthy, but he shall fall in sickhess.'   θῆναι, ἀλλὰ πεσεῖται νόσῳ.

Job cries out that he himself longs to find God but that God is nowhere to be
found.

Bildad, in trying to answer this outburst of Job, very briefly
states in chapter 25 as the majesty of God is true, so is the impossibility
of any man's being considered as just or pure before God. He says that even
the moon has no brightness independent of God. Furthermore he states (M 25:5b):

'And the stars are not pure in his eyes.' וכוכבים לא־זכו בעיניו

As in the Hebrew of 15:5b the translator may have understood בעיניו in a
figurative sense, but he avoids any possible anthropomorphism by rendering
בעיניו as ἐναντίον αὐτοῦ 'before him'. G reads:

'And stars are not pure before him.' ἄστρα δὲ οὐ καθαρὰ ἐναντίον αὐτοῦ.

After Job 's reply to Bildad (chaps. 26-27) there comes in chapter
28 a poem filled with rich imagery and figures drawn from the world of nature.
The limitations of finite knowledge in contrast to the transcendence of in-
finite wisdom are set forth. God is represented as cognizant of the entire
realm of nature.[1] M 28:10b reads concerning God:

'And every precious thing his eye seeth.' וכל־יקר ראתה עינו

----

[1]Whether chap. 28 is an independent poem or an integral part of Job's
discourse is a problem still open to discussion. Cf., Bernhaad Duhm, *Das Buch
Hiob*, Vol. 16 of *Kurzer Hand-Commentar zum Alten Testament*, ed. Karl Marti

Both Codex Alexandrinus and Codex Sinaiticus read αὐτοῦ ὁ ὀφθαλμός 'his eye'

for עֵינוֹ 'his eye'. Codex Vaticanus, however, which most closely represents

the Old Greek reads μου ὁ ὀφθαλμός 'mine eye'. This latter reading would re-

fer to the poet himself. It is unlikely that there is inner Greek corruption

here and that Vaticanus is wrong in its reading μου. Paleographically it is

impossible to confuse the following readings:

ΜΟΥ 'my' Codex Vaticanus
ΑΥΤΟΥ 'his' Codices Alexandrinus and Sinaiticus.

The text of Grabe follows the reading αὐτοῦ ὁ ὀφθαλμός.[1] The text of Rahlfs

reads μου ὁ ὀφθαλμός.[2] In light of the examples already cited in this chap-

ter the writer concludes that the reading αὐτοῦ ὁ ὀφθαλμός 'his eye' does

not represent the Old Greek; it is a later correction of the Greek upon the

basis of the Hebrew. G merely wished to avoid the anthropomorphism of עֵינוֹ

'his eye'. The translator therefore employed a simple trick of translation,

reading as ו as י to obtain עֵינִי 'mine eye'. G reads as follows:

'And every prized thing mine eye (i.e., the   πᾶν δὲ ἔντιμον ἴδεν μου ὁ ὀφθαλμός·
poet's eye) hath seen.'

Although the tendency of the translator to avoid expressing the

action of God in human terms is especially noticeable in connection with the

word עַיִן 'eye', it also occurs when other bodily terms such as 'head', 'face',

'mouth', 'hands', or 'breath' are used in Hebrew.

Sophar in his first speech to Job (chap. 11) protests against that

which he considers as self-righteousness on the part of Job. He says (M 11:5)::

(Freiburg: Verlag von J. C. B. Mohr (Paul Siebeck), p. 134; Driver and Gray,
op. cit., I, 232-36; Budde, op. cit., pp. 155-57; Dhorme, op. cit., pp. xli-
xlii, lxxvi.

[1]Cf., Grabe, op. cit., ad loc.

[2]Cf., Rahlfs, op. cit., ad loc.

'But oh that God would speak   ואולם מי־יתן אלוה דבר
And open his lips with thee!'   ויפתח שפתיו עמך

The translator wishes to avoid the concept that it would be possible or desirable for God to speak directly to man. He therefore changes line 1 from a wish to a question. He objects, moreover, to the anthropomorphic expression יפתח שפתיו of line 2, and accordingly omits the line. G reads:

'But how would the Lord speak to thee?' ἀλλὰ πῶς ἂν ὁ κύριος λαλήσαι πρὸς σέ;

Job attempts to show that he is blameless in his observance of the law of God (chap. 23). He insists that he has followed the ways of God (M 23: 11-12):

'My foot hath held fast to his (God's) steps.   באשרו אהזה רגלי
His way have I kept and turned not aside.   דרכו שמרתי ולא־אט
I have not gone back from the commandments of his lips.   מצות שפתיו ולא אמיש
More than my law I have treasured up the words of his mouth.'   מחקי צפנתי אמרי־פיו

The translator objects to the anthropomorphic expressions באשרו 'to his steps', שפתיו 'his lips', and פיו 'his mouth'. He therefore interprets באשרו as ἐν ἐν~άλμασιν αὐτοῦ 'in his commandments' and omits שפתיו and פיו. G also avoids the words מחקי 'more than my law' (i. e., the law of conscience in contrast to God's law) in connection with a law of man, since חק is used for the statutes of God as seen in reference to the Ten Commandments.[1] He plays with the words, reading ב 'in' for מ 'from' and חקי as 'my bosom' instead of 'my law'. G accordingly reads:

'For I shall go forth in his commandments;   ἐξελεύσομαι δὲ ἐν ἐντάλμασιν αὐτοῦ,
His ways have I kept, and I will not turn   ὁδοὺς γὰρ αὐτοῦ ἐφύλαξα, καὶ οὐ μὴ
aside.   ἐκκλίνω·
I will even not pass by from his command-   ἀπὸ ἐνταλμάτων αὐτοῦ καὶ οὐ μὴ παρ-
ments,   έλθω,
But in my bosom I have hid his words.'   ἐν δὲ κόλπῳ μου ἔκρυψα ῥήματα αὐτοῦ.

---

[1] חק is used in the sense of Law in Exod. 12:24; עולם חק Exod. 29:28; 30:21; Lev. 6:11. חק in the sense of 'laws of God, commandments' is found in Exod. 18:16; Deut. 4:5, 8, 14; 6:24; 11:32; 12:1; Ps. 50:16, etc. Duhm, op. cit., p. 120, and Budde, op. cit. p. 132, read with the LXX בחקי. It is possible, however, to render מחקי as 'more than my portion'.

These examples clearly show that the translator was governed by a tendency to eschew anthropomorphisms, [1] but that he did not deliberately set out to elimin - ate all such expressions.

In his second speech (chap. 15) Eliphaz depicts the certain doom of the wicked. He asserts that the tyrannical man may be rich and prosperous, but that his wealth vanishes as quickly as a tree ruined by lightning. The end of such an one is described by Eliphaz as follows (M 15:30c):

'And he departs by the breath of his (God's) mouth.' ויסור ברוח פיו

The translator objects to the expression ברוח פיו as applied to God and there- fore substitutes another form of death:

'But let his (the wicked's) blossom drop off.' ἐκπέσοι δὲ αὐτοῦ τὸ ἄνθος.

In his long harangue on the goodness of God Elihu extols the works of God in nature. He says (M37:10):

'By the breath of God ice is given, מנשמת־אל יתן־קרח
And the breadth of the waters is straitened? ורחב מים במוצק

The translator omits the first line which contains the expression מנשמת־אל and renders the second line freely. He treats the noun רחב 'breadth' as a verb, rendering it as οἰακίζει 'he guides'. G may have played with the phrase במצק, treating it as כמועצה 'according to plan', rendering as ὡς ἐὰν βούληται 'as he may desire'. G reads:

'He guides the water just as he   οἰακίζει δὲ τὸ ὕδωρ ὡς ἐὰν βούληται·
may desire.'

Not only does the translator reject any depiction of God in human form with reference to parts of the body, but he also removes any portrayal of God with reference to his conforming to human behaviour:

----

[1]Cf., Gehman, *op. cit.*, p. 236, for a discussion of 4:9.

References to God as Conforming to Human

Behaviour Removed

In the passages which follow the translator removes the concepts
that 'God performs physical labour, that he acts as a human king with an army,
and that he is of corporeal substance which a man can see or touch. To achieve
this end G employs tricks of translation and plays on words. The result is a
rendering of the Hebrew which reflects the theological approach of the translator.

In the concluding section of his speech (chaps. 36-37) Elihu presents his interpretation of the right and the wrong way of accepting disciplinary suffering. Men who are afflicted should recognize that they have transgressed. They should learn from God who does not reject the innocent. The
Hebrew of M 36:5÷10 reads:

'Behold, God is mighty, yet he despiseth not any;	הֶן־אֵל כַּבִּיר וְלֹא יִמְאָס
He is mighty in strength of understanding.	כַּבִּיר כֹּחַ לֵב
He preserveth not the life of the wicked;	לֹא־יְחַיֶּה רָשָׁע
But giveth to the poor their right.	וּמִשְׁפַּט עֲנִיִּים יִתֵּן
He withdraweth not his eyes from the righteous;	לֹא־יִגְרַע מִצַּדִּיק עֵינָיו
But with kings upon the throne	וְאֶת־מְלָכִים לַכִּסֵּא
He setteth them forever and they are exalted.'	וַיֹּשִׁיבֵם לָנֶצַח וַיִּגְבָּהוּ
And if they be bound in fetters	וְאִם־אֲסוּרִים בַּזִּקִּים
And be caught' in the cords of affliction,	יִלָּכְדוּן בְּחַבְלֵי־עֹנִי
Then he declareth to them their work	וַיַּגֵּד לָהֶם פָּעֳלָם
And their transgressions, that they behave themselves proudly.	וּפִשְׁעֵיהֶם כִּי יִתְגַּבָּרוּ
He openeth also their ear to instruction	וַיִּגֶל אָזְנָם לַמּוּסָר
And commandeth that they return from iniquity.'	וַיֹּאמֶר כִּי־יְשֻׁבוּן מֵאָוֶן

In 'line 1 of verse 5 the translator felt the need of an object for יִמְאָס. He therefore played with the word כַּבִּיר, reading it as בְּבַר, The first בְּ then is treated
as the sign of the object of the verb מאס and בר 'blameless' is translated as
ἄκακον. G accordingly renders in such a way as to magnify the grace of God,
who does not reject the blameless. G then eliminates the anthropomorphic use of
לֵב (vs. 5b) and עֵינָיו (vs. 7) as applied to God and removes the mechanical details

of God's work by omitting verses 5b-9. G further objects to the concept that

God would physically open a man's ear (vs. 10) even though for instruction.

Although the Greek translator understands the symbolic use of וְיִגֶל אָזְנָם, he

plays with the words in such a way as to present the less objectionable con-

cept of God's opening his own ear. He therefore renders וְיִגֶל אָזְנָם as εἰσακούσεται

'he hearkens unto', and by reading the root יָשַׁר 'be upright' instead of יֹסֵר in

מוֹסֵר, he obtains τοῦ δικαίου 'the just' which is governed by εἰσακούσεται. G

thus obtains a logical sequence of thought from the first line of verse 5 to

verse 10a with the result that it magnifies the grace of God. G reads:

'But know ye that the Lord will not reject   γίγνωσκε δὲ ὅτι ὁ κύριος οὐ μὴ ἀπο-
              the one who is blameless;   ποιήσηται τὸν ἄκακον,
But he will hearken to the just one.'   ἀλλὰ τοῦ δικαίου εἰσακούσεται·

In the prose of the epilogue to Job (M 42:7-17) God says that his

condemnation of the three friends is to be assuaged through Job's intercession

on their behalf. Thus God directs Eliphaz, Bildad, and Sophar (M 42:8):

'And let my servant Job pray for you;   וְאִיּוֹב עַבְדִּי יִתְפַּלֵּל עֲלֵיכֶם
for him will I accept that I do no   כִּי אִם־פָּנָיו אֶשָּׂא לְבִלְתִּי עֲשׂוֹת
foolish thing to you;'   עִמָּכֶם נְבָלָה

G wishes to avoid so degrading a concept of God as that of his performing נְבָלָה.

He therefore changes to a condition contrary to fact and renders:

'But my servant Job will pray for you;   'Ιὼβ δὲ ὁ θεράπων μου   εὔξεται περὶ ὑμῶν,
for had it not been for him, I should   εἰ μὴ γὰρ δι' αὐτόν, ἀπώλεσα ὑμᾶς·
have destroyed you.'

The concept that God would destroy apparently was less objectionable to the

translator than the suggestion that God might effect something stupid or foolish.

The translator also eliminates concepts of God which portray him as

acting like a human king with an army. When Job replies to Bildad's first

speech (chaps. 9-10), he reflects upon the apparent contradictoriness of God's

action in afflicting him. Job complains to God (M 10:17):

'Thou renewest thy witnesses before me   תְּחַדֵּשׁ עֵדֶיךָ נֶגְדִּי

And increasest thy vexation against me; וְתֶרֶב כַּעַשְׂךָ עִמָּדִי
Columns and a host (come) against me.' חֲלִיפוֹת וְצָבָא עִמִּי

It seems that G objects to God's having witnesses to support his treatment of
Job. The translator, therefore, omits the ך from עֵדֶיךָ 'thy witnesses' to obtain עֵדִי 'my witness' which he renders as τὴν ἔτασίν μου 'mine affliction',[1]
G further alters line 2 to avoid the unflattering picture of God's multiplying
vexation against Job. G chose rather to portray God as thundering in wrath
against Job. G then avoids the physical connotation of 'columns and host'
with respect to God, rendering חֲלִיפוֹת וְצָבָא עִמִּי as πειρατήρια trials, temptations'.[2] G accordingly reads:

'Renewing upon me mine affliction; ἐπανακαινίζων ἐπ' ἐμὲ τὴν ἔτασίν μου·
And in great wrath thou hast dealt with me, ὀργῇ δὲ μεγάλῃ μοι ἐχρήσω,
And thou didst bring trials upon me.' ἐπήγαγες δὲ ἐπ' ἐμὲ πειρατήρια.

In his reply to Bildad's second speech, Job (chap. 19) recounts the
misfortunes which have befallen him, the scorn and hatred manifested toward
him by his former friends. He wishes that he had some permanent record of his
words. He does, however, maintain that his גֹּאֵל 'vindicator, redeemer' lives
who will stand as witness to his innocence. The Hebrew reads (M 19:25-27):

'But I know that my vindicator liveth. וַאֲנִי יָדַעְתִּי גֹּאֲלִי חָי
And at the last he will rise up upon the dust; וְאַחֲרוֹן עַל־עָפָר יָקוּם
And after my skin they have torn away thus, וְאַחַר עוֹרִי נִקְּפוּ־זֹאת
Then apart from my flesh I shall see God, וּמִבְּשָׂרִי אֶחֱזֶה אֱלוֹהַּ
Whom I shall see for myself; אֲשֶׁר אֲנִי אֶחֱזֶה־לִּי
And mine eyes shall behold and not another; וְעֵינַי רָאוּ וְלֹא־זָר
My reins are consumed within me.' כָּלוּ כִלְיֹתַי בְּחֵקִי

----

[1]It may be that עֵדִי 'my witness' suggests the idea of inquisition,
whence τὴν ἔτασίν μου 'mine affliction'. Cf., Schleusner, op. cit., s.v., ἔτασις.
At any rate in G ἔτασιν, ὀργῇ, and πειρατήρια are parallel.

[2]צָבָא in Isa. 40:2 is used in the sense of 'discipline, instruction'.
The more natural meaning of πειρατηρια as 'trials, temptations' better fits the
context than 'hordes of pirates' favoured by Gerleman, op. cit., p. 37. Gerleman
lists Job 7:1, 10:17, and 19:12 as proofs that πειρατηρια must mean 'horde of pirates'. Such a meaning, however, is out of context in 7:1 (where the Greek clearly refers to the trials which beset a man) and in 10:17 (discussed above). In
7:1 and 10:17 πειρατηρια is chosen by the translator to render צָבָא. In 19:12, however, as in 25:3 (not cited by Gerleman) πειρατηρια renders גְּדוּד, with the meaning
'horde of pirates'. Gerleman compares these examples with Job 16:10 (a weak case,

The interpretation of this passage has long been subject to debate. The text
itself is difficult; the context, ambiguous.[1] In M 14:14 Job, in asking whether a man who dies will live again, clearly expects the answer 'No'. The
passage cited above may be interpreted in one of two ways: (a) a *post mortem* point of view, or (b) an *ante mortem* point of view.

The *post mortem* point of view implies a resurrection after death.
גאלי חי would denote God who lives, though Job be dead. In this case אחרון
would refer to a point of time in an eschatological era; עפר, to Job's grave;
אחר עורי, to the dissolution of Job's body; and נקפו זאת, to the work of·
heavenly powers.[2] The words נקפו זאת, however, present a serious problem.
The *post mortem* explanation of the verses demands that the indefinite subject
of נקפו be interpreted with the same meaning as above. The use of זאת is to be
taken as adverbial, 'thus'.[3] Origen supports a *post mortem* exegesis of the
passage and so do the majority of interpreters in the Eastern Church from the
time of Chrysostom on.[4] Codices Sinaiticus and Alexandrinus for עורי 'my skin'
read μου τὸ σῶμα 'my body' by synecdoche, thus supporting a resurrection of
the body.[5]

----

since G departs from a literal rendering of the Hebrew) and Gen. 49:19 (where
the verb גוד is rendered by πειρατηρια to mean 'trials, temptations, when representing צבא and 'brigands, hordes of pirates' when representing גדוד

[1]From the context זר (vs. 27) may well be rendered as a possessive:
'another's.'

[2]Arnold B. Ehrlich, *Randglossen zur Hebräischen Bibel*, Vol. VI,
Psalmen, Sprüche und Hiob (Leipzig: J.C.Hinrichs'sche Buchhandlung, 1918), p. 257.

[3]For this adverbial use of זאת and זה, cf., M 19:3 זה עשר פעמים 'Ten
times now. . .

[4]Cf. Julius Speer, 'Zur Exegese von Hiob 19:25-27,' *Zeitschrift für
die Alttestamentliche Wissenschaft*, XXV (1905), 47-140, for a discussion of the
history of the interpretation of this passage.

[5]Cf. Gerleman, *op. cit.*, pp. 61-2.

The *ante mortem* point of view implies no resurrection. According to this interpretation גאל חי would refer to God, who, in contrast to Job, lives forever; אחרון, to a time in the future when God will show Job as innocent before all men; על־עפר יקום, to God's standing upon the earth as witness for Job; אחר עורי, to Job's life which remains within him (אחר in the temporal sense of 'behind', like Arabic سعى);[1] נקפו זאת, to the ravages of disease which have 'thus' torn Job's skin.[2]

It is the opinion of the writer that Job speaks from an *ante mortem* point of view. It may be that his suffering has deprived him of reason so that he is driven into a trance or coma in which he sees God as justifying his suffering.[3] Verse 26 is then to be rendered as above, with the meaning that after the torments of his disease have driven him into a trance, he, being disembodied (מבשרי), sees God for himself.

Hellenistic-Jewish circles at work on this passage, however, treat the passage in the following manner. G objects to גאל חי on the basis that God does not 'live' in the sense that a man lives. He therefore joins these words to the following אחרון and renders as ἀενός ἐστιν ὁ ἐκλύειν με μέλλων 'eternal is he who is about to release me', with μέλλων representing the root אחר. G avoids the possibility that God or heavenly powers could be the subject of נקפו (vs. 26) by treating the verb as singular reflexive, referring to

----

[1]Cf., Budde, *op. cit.*, pp. 105-6; Ehrlich, *op. cit.*, p. 257.

[2]But compare the discussions by Duhm, *op. cit.*, p. 103, Budde, *op. cit.*, pp. 106-7, Ehrlich, *op. cit.*, p. 267, and Driver and Gray, *op. cit.*, II, 129-33.

[3]But cf., C. Bruston, 'Pour l'exégèse de Job 19, 25-29,' *Zeitschrift fur die Alttestamentliche Wissenschaft*, XXVI (1906), 143-46. Bruston maintains that Job describes a vision of God who vindicates him in the future when he is dead and no longer conscious.

עורי. 'קום of verse 25 is then taken as the main verb for verse 26 which is rendered as ἀναστήσει τὸ δέρμα μου τὸ ἀνατλῶν ταῦτα. זאת is rendered twice in verse 26 by ταῦτα 'these things'. The translator then construes מבשרי 'apart from my flesh' (in the sense of 'my person') as μοι and by reading the root היה instead of חזה in אחזה 'I shall see', he obtains ταῦτά μοι συνετελέσθη 'these happened to me'. G further avoids the concept of verse 27c that Job's reins are consumed. He treats כלו 'they are consumed' as כל which he renders πάντα 'all'. He then plays with the noun כליתי 'my reins', reading it as a verb from the root כלה which he renders as συνετελέσθη. G therefore reads:

'For I know that eternal is he who is about to release me on earth;	οἶδα γὰρ ὅτι ἀέναός ἐστιν ὁ ἐκ-λύειν με μέλλων ἐπὶ γῆς
He would raise my skin that is suffering these things;	ἀναστήσαι τὸ δέρμα μου τὸ ἀναντλοῦν ταῦτα.
For from the Lord these things happened to me;	παρὰ γὰρ Κυρίου ταῦτά μοι συνε-τελέσθη,
Which (things) I understand for myself,	ἃ ἐγὼ ἐμαυτῷ συνεπίσταμαι,
Which mine eye has seen, and not another;	ἃ ὁ ὀφθαλμός μου ἑόρακεν καὶ οὐκ ἄλλο
But all these have happened to me, within me.	πάντα δέ μοι συντετέλεσται ἐν κόλπῳ.

The Greek rendering is ambiguous, but no more so than the original. Verse 25 depicts God as eternal, and Job's release from suffering as an earthly one. It may also be interpreted as meaning release from earth and resurrection of the body (skin). The rendering of verse 26 is also ambiguous. A probable inter-pretation is that Job in the future (so line 1) will understand God's treat-ment of him. But line 2 implies that Job already has understood God's purposes. There can be no objection to taking both the Hebrew and the Greek as pertain-ing to a trance in which Job has had a vision of God's purposes for him. Cer-tainly the emphatic assertion of Job in the Hebrew that he and he alone 'has seen' can logically pertain to such a vision.[1] One fact is certain: G avoids

----

[1] The use of the verbs חזה and ראה in M 19:26-27 supports the con-cept of 'vision, trance' and is reminiscent of the frenzied seer in the history of Old Testament prophecy.

the anthropomorphic concept of any man's seeing God, even though it be applied
to a vision. Job understands his plight and sees his condition in the light
of God's purposes.

When Elihu tries to convince Job that he is foolish to blame God
for his misfortunes (chap..35), he says (M 35:13-14):

Surely God will not hear vanity;   אך־שוא לא־ישמע אל
Nor will the Almighty behold it.   ושדי לא ישורנה
How much less, when thou sayest thou canst not see him!   אף כי־תאמר לא תשורנו
The cause is before him (God); therefore, wait thou for him.'   דין לפניו ותחולל לו

The translator objects to the implication that God does not hear or see all
things. He therefore changes the first verb in verse 13 to one of seeing and
adds βούλεται, rendering the line to show that God does not wish to see wicked
things. He omits the second לא of the verse,,thereby portraying God as one
who sees. G treats לא תשורנו (vs..14) as לא ישר 'not upright', rendering it as
τὰ ἄνομα 'wrong things'. The place of אף כי־תאמר in line 1 of verse 14 is oc-
cupied in G by τῶν συντελούντων 'of those who bring about, effect', which does
not render the Hebrew. It appears that the translator deliberately changed
אף כי־תאמר for the sake of the sense. It is possible that אמר suggested to
him גמר 'bring to an end, complete', whence he could have obtained something
like the rendering of G. The translator then adds the phrase καὶ σώσει με,
in this way magnifying the grace of God. By this method the translator avoids
the concept, even though stated negatively, that a man may see God. G then
treats דין 'cause' as a verb and renders it as κρίθητι 'be brought to trial',
He eliminates the picture of Job's waiting for God as if for a human judge, by
playing with תחלל 'wait thou!', reading the ח of תחלל as ה, which yields
תהלל 'praise thou!'. This he renders by the verb αἰνέω 'praise'. G accordingly reads:

'For the Lord does not wish to see wicked things; ἄτοπα/γὰρ οὐ βούλεται ὁ κύριος
                                                                                    ἰδεῖν·

For the Almighty himself is a beholder αὐτὸς γὰρ ὁ παντοκράτωρ ὁρατής ἐστιν
Of those who effect wrong things, and me τῶν συντελούντων τὰ ἄνομα, καὶ σώσει
    will he save.   με.
But be thou brought to trial before him, κρίθητι δὲ ἐναντίον αὐτοῦ
    if thou art able to praise him as   εἰ δύνασαι αἰνέσαι αὐτὸν
    he is.'   ὡς ἔστιν.

        The translator also eliminates anthropomorphisms which refer to the

expression 'sons of God' or to the concept of human emotions and mental process-

es as applied to God.

The Removal of References to 'Sons of God'

and to Human Emotions or Mental

Processes as Applied to God

        In the first chapter of Job the translator eliminates the portrayal

of God in human terms by avoiding any implication of God's having children. In

the introductory prose section of the book, the scene of the angels before God

is depicted. M goes as follows (1:6):

'And there was a day when the sons of God came ויהי היום ויבאו בני האלהים
to present themselves before Yahweh;' להתיצב על־יהוה

G realizes that בני אלהים denotes 'sons of divinity, sons of deity' and does

not refer to the human concept of son. The translator does object, however,

to the possibility that בני אלהים could have a mythological connotation and

thereby undermine the Old Testament concept of monotheism. He therefore changes

to οἱ ἄγγελοι τοῦ θεοῦ 'the angels of God' and renders:

'And when there came this (certain) day. then Καὶ ὡς ἐγένετο ἡ ἡμέρα αὕτη,
behold! -- the angels of God came to stand be- καὶ ἰδοὺ ἦλθον οἱ ἄγγελοι τοῦ θεοῦ
fore the Lord;' παραστῆναι ἐνώπιον τοῦ κυρίου.

The translator also renders בני אלהים by οἱ ἄγγελοι τοῦ θεοῦ in the parallel

passage of the Hebrew for 2:1.

        A similar treatment of this phrase is found in God's address to

Job (chap. 38). When he chides Job for attempting to penetrate the mystery of

God's ways, he asks him where he was at the creation of the world, thereby

implying that Job could not possibly understand so deep a mystery. God says

that it was at that time (M 38:7-8):

'When the morning stars sang together,	ברן־יחד כוכבי בקר
And all the sons of God shouted for joy?	ויריעו כל־בני אלהים
When he shut up the sea with doors;	ויסך בדלתים ים
When it broke forth and issued out of the womb;'	בגיחו מרחם יצא

Once again G eliminates the objectionable words **בני אלהים** by rendering them as

ἄγγελοί μου . G then changes from the third to the first person in verse 8 to

preserve a consistent seouence of the first person pronoun throughout the first

eleven verses of the chapter. G is more matter-of-fact and evades the rhetori-

cal question in M. That G retains the figure of God's fencing in the sea with

a gate is but one more proof that the translator does not adhere to any mechani-

cal system of exegesis but that he merely follows a tendency toward removing

anthropomorphisms. G reads:

'When the stars came into being, all my angels	ὅτε ἐγενήθησαν ἄστρα, ἤνεσάν
praised me with loud voice;	με φωνῇ μεγάλῃ πάντες ἄγγε-
And I fenced in the sea with gates,	λοί μου. ἔφραξα δὲ θάλασσαν
When it trembled, coming forth from its mother's womb.	πύλαις, ὅτε ἐμαίμασσεν ἐκ κοι-
	λίας μητρὸς αὐτὴ ἐκπορευομένη·

The translator not only eliminates the possibility of misinterpreting

בני אלהים, but also removes the portrayal of God as having human emotions or as

conforming to human mental processes. He therefore departs from a literal ren-

dering of the Hebrew in those passages which depict God as arousing himself or

as rising up in judgment.

When Bildad first addresses Job, he exhorts him to learn from the

past that God rewards the righteous and punishes the ungodly. He tells Job

that if he is pure and upright, God will respond to him (M 8:6b):

'Surely now he (God) will arouse himself on thy behalf.' כי־עתה יעיר עליך

The translator does not like the anthropomorphic concept of God's arousing himself and accordingly renders:

'He will hearken unto thine entreaty.' δεήσεως ἐπακούσεταί σου.

Job may have had the words of Bildad in mind when he delivered his

closing monologue (chaps. 29-31). He states that if he had rejected the rights

of his servants (M 31:14a):

'What then shall I do when God riseth up?' ומה אעשה כי־יקום אל

Again the translator eschews the figure of God's rising up in the fashion of

a man, and accordingly he renders the verse as follows:

'For what shall I do if the Lord will make an τί γὰρ ποιήσω ἐὰν ἔτασίν μου
    examination of me?'   ποιῆται ὁ κύριος;

The examples cited in this chapter prove that the translator employs

anti-anthropomorphisms. It would be wrong to assume, however, that G conforms

to a rigid or mechanical system of removing every representation of God in hu-

man form, for the translator of Job realized that any representation of God

must be expressed in terms of human understanding. Whenever G resorts to anti-

anthropomorphisms, it does so to exalt the concept of God in accordance with

the theology prevailing in Hellenistic-Jewish circles. The theological use of

anti-anthropomorphisms is therefore an integral part of the exegetical method

of the Greek translator of the Book of Job.

CHAPTER III

DETRACTION FROM THE PERFECT CHARACTER

OF GOD AVOIDED

In addition to following a theological method of toning down certain
passages of the Hebrew text and of employing anti-anthropomorphisms, the translator avoids expressions which may not appear commendatory in reference to God.
The means by which G achieves this end vary. The translator does not always
omit the name of God from an objectionable context, but he does attempt to
soften any description of God which detracts from an elevated concept of his
attributes or actions. In some places G eliminates such a description. In
other instances the translator plays with the Hebrew words or roots in order
to improve upon a statement concerning God. The first section of this chapter,
therefore, deals with the following theme:

Descriptions of God Which Are

Avoided or Changed

In chapter 6 of the Hebrew text Job replies to the first speech of
Eliphaz. In order to elicit the sympathy of Eliphaz, Bildad, and Sophar Job
describes his sufferings, saying that his friends should not condemn him,
since God is the author of his afflictions.[1]

The more Job considers his position, the more unjust he feels his
calamities to be. In chapter 7 he breaks forth into a pathetic cry of despair,
longing for death. He accuses God of allowing him no respite even for one

----

[1]For a discussion of 6:4c, cf., Gehman, op. cit., p. 235.

brief moment. Job cries out (M 7:20):

'If I have sinned, what do I unto thee, O thou   חטאתי מה אפעל לך
       keeper of man?   נצר האדם
Why hast thou set me as a thing for thee to   למה שמתני
       strike against,   למפגע לך
So that I am a burden to myself?'   ואהיה עלי למשא

G removes the possibility, even thou stated negatively, that a man could do anything to God, by adding to the first line δύναμαι 'I am able'. The translator then changes the rather unflattering description of God from that of a keeper or warden to that of one who understands the mind of man. In the second line of the Hebrew God is represented as discriminating against Job. G reverses the idea so that Job asks why he is established as an accuser of God. The reading עלי of M in line 3 is one of eighteen alterations made by the scribes in the original texts (תיקון סופרים).[1] The original reading of עלי was עליך 'unto thee (God)'.[2] The scribes, however, apparently believed that describing anyone as a משא 'burden' to God was impious and therefore changed to עלי by omitting the ך of עליך. G apparently believes that line 2 is more objectionable in the Hebrew than the reading עליך in line 3. It therefore renders line 2 as discussed above and retains the reading of the original Hebrew text which was later changed by Jewish scribes. Accordingly it renders עליך as ἐπί σοί in line 3. G reads:

'If I have sinned, what am I able to do   εἰ ἐγὼ ἥμαρτον, τί δύναμαί σα πρᾶξαι,
       unto thee,
Thou who understandest the mind of men?   ὁ ἐπιστάμενος τὸν νοῦν τῶν ἀνθρώπων;
Why hast thou set me as thine accuser?   διὰ τί ἔθουυμε κατεντευκτήν σου,
So that I am a burden to thee?'   εἰμὶ δὲ ἐπὶ σοὶ φορτίον;

     Like Bildad Sophar bluntly attacks Job in his first speech (chap. 11).

----

[1]Christian D. Ginsburg, *Introduction to the Massoretico-Critical Edition of the Hebrew Bible* (London: Trinitarian Bible Society, 1897), p. 360.

[2]Cf., Kennicott and De Rossi, *op. cit., ad loc.*

He calls Job a scoffer and self-righteous transgressor. He maintains that the ways of God are beyond human comprehension. If God, knowing how men have sinned, chooses to bring them to judgment, they cannot call him back (M 11:10):

'If he (God) pass through and imprison,   אם־יחלף ויסגיר
And call an assembly, then who can turn him back?'   ויקהיל ומי ישיבנו

G objects, however, to the idea of imprisonment and a judgment hall or assembly as applied to the action of God. It therefore changes the figure by rendering אם־יחלף 'if he pass through' freely as ἐὰν καταστρέψη 'if he overturn', a meaning easily derived from the Hiphil. The root סגר of ויסגר 'and he imprison' suggests the idea of inclusion, so G renders it as τὰ πάντα 'everything'. The translator also avoids the reference in line 2 of the Hebrew that a person could restrain God, even though the implied answer is negative. He therefore understands ישיבנו 'one can turn him (God) back' in the sense of answering him and renders, 'Who will say to him?'. Finally G quotes Job's question (in M 9:12) מה־תעשה 'What dost thou do?'. G reads

'If he overturn everything,   ἐὰν δὲ καταστρέψη τὰ πάντα,
Who will say to him, What dost thou do?' τίς ἐρεῖ αὐτῷ Τί ἐποίησας;

Job ironically replies to Bildad that he knows that his three friends are the embodiment of wisdom and that when they die wisdom will die also. He then tells them that the facts of life lend no support to their platitudes. He cites the example of unpunished wicked (M 12:6):

'The tents of robbers prosper,   ישליו אהלים לשדדים
And there is security to those who provoke God,   ובטחות למרגיזי אל
According as one who brings God in his hand.' לאשר הביא אלוה בידו

The concept of the Hebrew that God acts capriciously is objectionable to the translator. He therefore begins at ובטחות 'and security' in line 2 of the Hebrew and reads backwards: ובטחות is represented by πεποιθέτω 'let him trust'; לשדדים 'of robbers', by πονηρὸς ὤν 'being evil'. אלהים is omitted. ישליו 'they prosper' is rendered by ἀθῷος ἔσεσθαι 'to be scot-free'. G then intro-

duces the negative οὐ μὴν δὲ ἀλλὰ μηδείς 'nevertheless, no one' into line 1
in order to avoid the idea that one may provoke God with impunity. G renders
למרניזי אל 'to those who provoke God' of line 2 of the Hebrew by ὅσοι παρορ-
γίζουσιν τὸν κύριον 'those who arouse the Lord to anger', with the ὅσοι clause
placed in apposition to μηδείς of line 1. The heathenish suggestion of line 3
that one could carry God like an idol in his hand is also eliminated. The
Hebrew of line 3 is difficult. G therefore assumes great freedom in rendering
it. לאשר 'as regards' is rendered by ὡς 'as'. הביא 'one brings' is treated
as a Qal and rendered by ἔσται 'it will be, come to pass'. אלוה is interpreted as אלה 'these things' and accordingly rendered as ἔτασις 'affliction'. As
in line 1 the translator adds a negative (οὐχί) according to context. בידו
'in his hand' is treated in the sense of 'upon him'. In line 1 of the Greek
the number is singular (μηδείς), but in line 2, it is plural (ὅσοι). G therefore interprets בידו freely as αὐτῶν 'their'. By employing the above method
the translator gives a meaning which opposite that of the Hebrew.[1] G reads:

'Nevertheless, let no one, being evil,	οὐ μὴν δὲ ἀλλὰ μηδεὶς πεποιθέτω πονη-
have trust that he will be scot-free,	ρὸς ὧν ἀθῷος ἔσεσθαι,
Those who arouse the Lord to anger,	ὅσοι παροργίζουσιν τὸν κύριον,
(Thinking) that even their affliction will	ὡς οὐχὶ καὶ ἔτασις αὐτῶν ἔσται.
not come to pass.'	

Job takes exception to the arguments of Eliphaz (M 5:4) and Sophar
(M 20:10) in which they uphold the contention that God visits the iniquity of
the wicked upon their children. Job quotes Eliphaz and Sophar as saying
(M 21:19a):

'God layeth up his (the wicked's) iniquity for   אלוה יצפן־לבניו אונו
his children.'

---

[1] Dhorme, op. cit., ad loc., maintains that the translator has built
up a free rendering around ובני. Gerleman, op. cit. p. 54, has missed the
point in stating concerning this verse, 'The verbose Greek version is probably
a paraphrase without exact correspondence in the original.

The idea   that God harbours punishment for the children of guilty fathers is
removed by the translator. He omits the וֹן of אֱלֹוֹהַ, leaving אל 'not'.[1] By
taking יִשְׁפֹּן as Niphal and introducing the negative אל he renders the expression as ἐκλίποι 'let there fail' and interprets אָוֶן 'iniquity' as אֹון 'possess-
ion', which he translates as ὑπάρχοντα:

'Let his possessions fail (his) children.' ἐκλίποι υἱοὺς τὰ ὑπάρχοντα αὐτοῦ·
There is no guilt attached by the translator to the children because of the sins
of the father.

For the third time Eliphaz (chap. 22) inveighs against Job. He insists that God derives no advantage from men whether they be good or bad. He
advises Job to put away unrighteousness and to humble himself. If Job does so,
says Eliphaz, then he will have   the full measure of the Almighty's favour
(M 22:25b):

'And his (the Almighty's) splendour[2] will be silver   וכסף תועפות לך
      unto thee.'

The translator objects to the metaphor by which God's splendour is represented
as silver. He therefore changes the figure, showing God's deliverance of Job:

But he will render thee pure as   καθαρὸν δὲ ἀποδώσει σε ὥσπερ ἀργύριον
      refined silver.'   πεπυρωμένον.

Eliphaz cites as a benefit which Job may reap from penance the following
(M 22:28a):

'And thou wilt also decree a thing, and it will be   ותגזר־אומר ויקם לך
      established unto thee.'

----

[1]The reading אל is better metrically than אֱלֹוהַ. It may be that G
had אל in the Hebrew text which it used.

[2]The meaning of תועפות has been subject to debate. Brown-Driver-
Briggs and Gesenius-Buhl (s.v.), say that the meaning here is uncertain, but
offer (1) 'peak' (צ'); (2) 'horns of wild animals'; (3) 'silver heaps',
Budde, op. cit., ad loc., emends to תורתו 'his teaching'; Duhm, op. cit., ad
loc., to תושבח 'sign s on the stars'. The meaning adopted here is based upon
a suggestion made by F. Zolli, 'Note di Lessicografia Biblica,' Biblica, XXVII
(1946), 127-28, who cites תועפת in Sirach 45:7 as meaning cime splendenti or
cime visibili, lucenti.

In rendering this passage the translator again stresses the superiority of God over man. He renders תגזר 'thou shalt decree a thing' freely by ἀπο-καταστήσει, thus chaning from the second to the third person with God understood as subject of the action. He then plays with the words ויקם אמר, reading them as nouns יקום 'substance, being', and אמת 'truth', which he freely renders in reverse order as δίαιταν and δικαιοσύνης. G reads:

'He will restore for thee a way of life ἀποκαταστήσει δὲ σοι δίαιταν δικαιο-
      of righteousness.'   σύνης.

When Job in chapter 23 replies to the third speech of Eliphaz, he answers the request of Eliphaz[1] to return to God by saying (M 23:3):

'O that I knew where I might find him (God), מי־יתן ידעתי ואמצאהו
That I might come even to his dwelling.'   אבוא עד־תכונתו

In the first lime G renders מי־יתן ידעתי by reading מי literally as 'who?' (τίς) and יתן ידעתי as יתן ידעיו, the final ו being read by dittography for the ו which introduces ואמצאהו. The translator wishes to avoid the thought in line 2 that one may come to God's dwelling or that God has a physical dwelling place or tribunal. He accordingly treats תוכנות 'dwelling as if it were from the root תכן (Piel, 'to determine, mete out'; תֹּכֶן 'fixed quantity, measure') instead of from כון 'to dwell', and renders it freely as τέλος 'end, accomplishment'. G therefore reads:

'Who then would know that I might τίς δ' ἄρα γνοίη ὅτι εὕροιμι
    find him,[2]   αὐτὸν
And that I might come at last?'   καὶ ἔλθοιμι εἰς τέλος;

Job then says in the Hebrew that if he found God or his dwelling, he would present his argument before God (M 23:4a):

'I would set out my case before him.' אערכה לפניו משפט

(M 13:3b). [1]Cf., the similar treatment in Job's reply to Sophar's first speech

[2]The reading of G 'Who then would know?' is a Hebraism meaning 'O!'.

The translator eliminates לפניו probably because he objects to the abruptness

of the Hebrew in stating that a man could present his case before God. He

reads:

'I would speak mine own judgment.' εἴποιμι δὲ ἐμαυτοῦ κρίμα.

Job insists, however, that if he could lay his case before God, trusting in

his mercy, then God would hearken unto him. Job expects the answer 'No' as he

asks concerning God (M 23:6):

'Would he contend with me in the great-   הברב־כח יריב עמדי
        ness of his power?
Nay, but he would give heed unto me.'   לא אך־הוא ישם בי

The translator does not like יריב עמד in line 1 because it not only is anthro-

pomorphic, but it places God and Job on the same level. He therefore plays

with יריב עמד, by reading the ע of עמד as the first letter of the root עבר

'pass over', the ב and ר of the root ריב being interchanged and the י of ריב

being placed before עבר. The result is יעבר 'he will pass over, forgive',

which G translates with עמדי as ἐπελεύσεταί μοι. G reads:

'And if in much strength he will come upon   καὶ ἐν πολλῇ ἰσχύι ἐπελεύσεταί
        me,[1]   μοι·
Then he will not treat me with threatening.' εἶτα ἐν ἀπειλῇ μοι οὐ χρήσεται.

        In the introduction to the speech of Elihu (32:1-6a) the reason

for Elihu's indignation against Job is given. Elihu is angry for the follow-

ing reason (M 32:2c):

'. . . because he (Job) considered himself more   על־צדקו נפשו מאלהים
righteous than God.'

Throughout its translation G avoids disparaging descriptions of Job's atti-

tude toward God. The fact that the Hebrew here suggests that a man can be

---

[1]In M the first line is a question introduced by ה and the answer
is לא. In LXX usage εἰ may be employed in a negative sense like אם in a
negative oath. Accordingly this line may probably be better rendered: 'And
not in much strength will he come upon me.' This translation would clearly
bring out the fact that God will have mercy on Job.

more righteous than God also is eliminated by the translator. He therefore
changes the comparative מן to ἐναντίον 'before' and renders:

'. . . because he declared himself righteous   διότι ἀπέφηνεν ἑαυτὸν δίχαιον
      before God.'   ἐναντίον Κυρίου.

After Elihu recounts the failure of the three friends to convince
Job of his guilt, he declares that he is forced to speak. He claims to have
a share of knowledge. Depicting himself as an impartial observer to the argument, Elihu resolves to flatter no one. Moreover, he gives a reason for his
objective approach (M 32:22):

'For I know not how to give flattering titles: כי לא ידעתי אכנה
My Maker would soon take me away.'   כמעט ישאני עשני

G wishes to eliminate the irreverent idea of God in line 2. By playing with
עשני 'my Maker' and reading it as עש 'moth', the translator eschews the idea
that God would destroy Elihu. He accordingly renders:

'For I do not know (how) to stand in awe of   οὐ γὰρ ἐπίσταμαι θαυμάσαι
     a person;   πρόσωπα·
But if not, moths shall even devour me.'   εἰ δὲ μή, καὶ ἐμὲ σῆτες ἔδονται.

In chapter 33 Elihu attacks Job's assertion that he is innocent and
that God deliberately seeks occasions against him. Elihu asks Job why he insists that God never answers him. He implies thereby that Job has not been
attentive enough to hear God when he speaks (M 33:14):

'For God speaketh in one way,   כי־באחת ידבר־אל
Yea in two, though man perceives it not.'   ובשתים לא ישורנה

The assertion that one could pay no regard (לא ישורנה) when God speaks is
omitted by the translator who maintains that when God speaks one must perceive
it. G fills in the gap left by the omission of לא ישורנה, by placing the
first word of verse 15 (בחלום 'in a dream') at the end of verse 14. G accordingly reads:

'For in one way the Lord would speak,   ἐν γὰρ τῷ ἅπαξ λαλῆσαι ὁ κύριος,
Yea in two -- a dream.'   ἐν δὲ τῷ δευτέρῳ ἐνύπνιον.

Elihu then offers an explanation for the suffering which a man
undergoes. He insists that God afflicts a man in order to turn him from pride
and wickedness, even though such suffering brings a man to the brink of death.
At this point, Elihu continues, God will intervene (M 33:23-24):

'If there be for him (man) an angel[1]	אם־יש עליו מלאך
An intermediary, one of a thousand,[1]	מליץ אחד מני־אלף
To make known unto a man what is right for him;	להגיד לאדם ישרו
Then he (God)[2] is gracious unto him and saith,	ויחננו ויאמר
Deliver him[3] from going down to the pit;[4]	פדעהו מרדת שחת
I have found a ransom.'	מצאתי כפר

The meaning of the Hebrew as translated above is that God accepts the intercession of an angel on behalf of man. Such intercession is regarded as a
ransom for man's wickedness and delivers a man from death. The translator
rejects this idea that God would accept mediation by an angel. In line 1 of
verse 23, therefore, the translator makes מלאך plural and defines as θανατηφόροι 'death-dealing', thereby eliminating any possibility that God would
kill a man (as is implied in the Hebrew of vs. 24bc). In line 2 of verse 23
G takes the literal meaning of מליץ (Hiphil participle of the root ליץ, 'one
scorning, mocking') and by adding the negative οὐ μή renders it as οὐ μή τρώσῃ
'he will not wound, injure, kill'. G thus omits the idea of an intercessory
angel. The translator apparently wishes to stress the fact that a wicked man
must repent in order to achieve God's forgiveness. He therefore adds a line
(after vs. 23ab) which was not in the *Vorlage*. This added line (written in
italics below) introduces God as subject of the verbs which follow in verses

---

[1]Budde, *op. cit.*, *ad loc.*, omits מלאך and אחד מני־אלף 'one of a
thousand' by maintaining that מליץ refers to a human being, namely, to Elihu.

[2]So Duhm, *op. cit.*, *ad loc.*; but Budde, *op. cit.*, *ad loc.*, says,
'Der Engel legt bei Gott Fuerbitte fuer den Menschen ein.'

[3]Both Duhm and Budde, *op. cit.*, *ad loc.*, read פרעהו 'set free'.

[4]Budde, *op. cit.*, *ad. loc.*, omits מרדת שחת as gloss, but adds נפשו

24 and 25. The translator apparently wishes to magnify the role of God in this passage, for he treats להגיד in line 3 of verse 23 as a finite verb (God as subject). By playing with ישׁר, reading it as מוסרו 'his correction', he renders as ἀναγγείλῃ δὲ ἀνθρώπῳ τὴν ἑαυτοῦ μέμψιν 'he will make known self-censure to a man'. G also represents a doublet in rendering להגיד לאדם ישׁרו (as is seen by l. 5 of vs. 23 in the Greek) as τὴν δὲ ἄνοιαν αὐτοῦ δείξῃ 'and his folly he will show him.' By pointing out to him what is right, God incidentally shows him his folly. G thus stresses the fact that man must recognize his own sinfulness..

G objects to the idea underlying the Hebrew of verses 23 and 24 that God is gracious because of the mediation of an angel. The translator has eliminated the figure of an intercessor between God and man, and he continues (in vs. 24) with God as subject of the verbs. He renders ויהננו freely as ἀνθέξεται 'he will take hold'. Τοῦ μὴ πεσεῖν 'so that he will not fall' represents מרדת, and θάνατος 'death' represents שׁחת. Then G obliterates the idea of a ransom in line 3 of verse 24. He treats כפר (root meaning 'cover') as ἀλοιφήν 'paint' and plays with מצאתי, reading the root מלא 'fill' which he renders as ἐμπλήσει 'he will fill'. The remainder of lines 2 and 3 in G represents an expansion of the first line of the Hebrew in verse 25: ἀνανεώσει 'he will renew' is for רטפשׁ 'become fresh'; αὐτοῦ τὸ σῶμα and τὰ ὀστὰ αὐτοῦ represent בשׁרו 'his flesh'. G accordingly renders verses 23 and 24:

'If there be a thousand death-dealing angels,[1]   ἐὰν ὦσιν χίλιοι ἄγγελοι θανατηφόροι
One of them will not kill him;   εἷς αὐτῶν οὐ μὴ τρώσῃ αὐτόν.
If he consider in his heart to turn to the Lord,   ἐὰν νοήσῃ τῇ καρδίᾳ ἐπιστραφῆναι
Then he (God) will make known self-censure to a   πρὸς Κύριον, ἀναγγείλῃ δὲ ἀνθρώπῳ
          man;   τὴν ἑαυτοῦ μέμψιν,

----

his soul' after ויהננו. Duhm, op. cit., ad loc., retains מרדת שׁחת but adds לנפשׁו 'for his soul' after כפר.

[1]Cf., infra, p. 59, for the possible reading of 'to the slayers' in vs. 22 as θανατηφόροι.

And his folly he will show him.	τὴν δὲ ἄνοιαν αὐτοῦ δείξῃ,
He will take hold (of him) so that he will not fall into death;	ἀνθέξεται τοῦ μὴ πεσεῖν εἰς θάνατον·
He will renew his body as paint upon a wall;	ἀνανεώσει δὲ αὐτοῦ τὸ σῶμα ὥσπερ·ἀλοιφὴν ἐπὶ τοίχου,
He will fill his bones with marrow.'	τὰ δὲ ὀστᾶ αὐτοῦ ἐμπλήσει μυελοῦ·

Elihu now delineates the result of intercession for the wicked.

He says (M 33:25-27):

'His flesh becometh fresh with youth; [1]	רטפש בשרו מנער
He returneth to the days of his youthful vigour.	ישוב לימי עלומיו
He prayeth unto God, and he (God) is favourable unto him;	יעתר אל־אלוה וירצהו
So that he seeth his (God's) face with joy;	וירא פניו בתרועה
And he (God) restoreth unto man his (man's) righteousness.	וישב לאנוש צדקתו
He (man) looketh upon men and saith:	ישר על־אנשים ויאמר
I have sinned and perverted that which was right,	חטאתי וישר העויתי
And it profiteth me not.' [2]	ולא־שוה לי

The translator, having shown in verses 23 and 24 that repentance secures the grace of God for the wicked, adheres to a more literal rendering of verses 25-27. In the second line of verse 26, however, he omits the ending וof פניו 'his (God's) face' to avoid the idea that any man may see the face of God. G, therefore, by a trick of the translator, interprets ירא as יבוא and renders εἰσελεύσεται δὲ προσώπῳ καθαρῷ, 'he (man) will enter with a pure countenance with utterance (of joy)', The translator also avoids the possibility that verse 27 of the Hebrew could be interpreted as meaning that God says he himself has sinned and turned right into wrong. G treats ישר על־אנשים in a free translation by concentrating upon אנשים and the idea of a penitent sinner. G accordingly renders as εἶτα τότε ἀπομέμψεται ἄνθρωπος αὐτὸς ἑαυτῷ 'accordingly then a man will personally rebuke himself'. In lines 3 and 4 of verse 27 G

---

[1]Budde, op. cit., ad loc., translates מנער as 'von Jugendfrische'; Duhm, op. cit. ad loc., as 'vor Jugendfrische'. If מן be taken as a comparative, מנער would yield '. . .than (that of) a youth.'

[2]Budde, op. cit., ad loc., wishes to add אל (God) to this line, reading ואין־לי 'but God did not requite it to me.'

makes clear that a man is a sinner whose good deeds do not atone for his evil

ones. וישר is represented by οἷα συνετέλουν 'whatever things I contributed,

brought about'; העויתי, by οὐκ ἤτασέν με 'did not afflict me'; ולא־שוה לי,

by καὶ ἄξια 'even sufficiently (to atone for)'; and החטאתי, by ὧν ἥμαρτον 'those

wherein I failed'. G accordingly reads:

'He (God) will make his (man's) flesh as tender as a child's;	ἀπαλυνεῖ δὲ αὐτοῦ τὰς σάρκας ὥσπερ νηπίου,
He will restore him reared into manhood (i.e., as a new man) among men.	ἀνανεώσει δὲ αὐτὸν ἀνδρωθέντα ἐν ἀνθρώποις.
But after he has prayed to the Lord, then matters will be acceptable unto him (God);	εὐξάμενος δὲ πρὸς Κύριον, καὶ δεκτὰ αὐτῷ ἔσται,
And he (man) will enter with a pure countenance with utterance (of joy);	εἰσελεύσεται δὲ προσώπῳ καθαρῷ σὺν ἐξηγορίᾳ·
Moreover he (God) will restore to men righteousness.	ἀποδώσει δὲ ἀνθρώποις δικαιοσύνην.
Accordingly then a man will personally rebuke himself, saying:	εἶτα τότε ἀπομέμψεται ἄνθρωπος αὐτὸς λέγων
Whatever things I contributed (brought about) did not afflict me even sufficiently (to atone for) those things wherein I failed.'	Οἷα συνετέλουν, καὶ οὐκ ἄξια ἤτασέν με ὧν ἥμαρτον.

Elihu had maintained that God uses suffering as a means of purging

sin from the wicked. The verses discussed above (33:23-27) describe the benefits which repentance brings a wicked man. There should be considered now the statements which Elihu makes in the Hebrew concerning the death of the evildoers.. These declarations of Elihu are not consistent within the following verses (M 33:22, 28-30):

Yea, his (the wicked's) soul draweth near to the pit;	ותקרב לשחת נפשו
And his life, to the slayers.	וחיתו לממתים
He (God) redeemeth my soul[1] from passing on to the pit,	פדה נפשי מעבר בשחת
And my life[1] seeth its fill of the light.	וחיתי באור תראה
Behold, all these things doth God work	הן־כל־אלה יפעל־אל
Twice, yea thrice, with a man,	פעמים שלוש עם־גבר

---

[1]The Ketīb is נפשי 'my soul' and חיתי 'my life'. The Qerā', however, reads נפשו 'his soul' and חיתו 'his life'. If the Ketīb is taken, as above, the line refers to Elihu who contrasts himself to the wicked. In vss. 29-30, however, 'man' is the subject treated, not Elihu. The reading which the Qerē' indicates would refer in vss. 28-30 to the wicked man.

To bring back his soul from the pit, להשיב נפשו מני־שחת
That he may be enlightened with the light of לאור באור החיים
the living.'

The translator follows the Hebrew of verse 22 rather carefully. He equates
θάνατος 'death' with שחת 'pit'. He certainly understood למתים to mean 'to
the slayers', but he made a better parallel to θάνατος by translating as ἐν
ἄδη 'in Hades'. In verse 23 of G θανατηφόροι occupies the place of מלץ. It
may be that in G's translation of verse 23 the interpretation of מלץ was
influenced by מתים in verse 22.[1] At any rate verse 22 in M portrays the
wicked man on the verge of death, while verse 22 in G depicts him as dead.
In the Hebrew of verse 28 (following the K^eṯîḇ of נפשי and חיתי) Elihu maintains that he is redeemed from death. But in verse 29 God is depicted as bringing a man's soul back from the pit to give him life again. In other words
the Hebrew of verse 22 depicts man as dying but not yet dead, whereas verse 30
implies that the man has died. The Hebrew is inconsistent. The translator
therefore makes a conflation of verses 28 and 30 of the Hebrew and places his
rendering in the position which verse 30 has in M. The part of verse 28 of
the Hebrew which G does not translate (מעבר בשחת), together with verse 29 is
omitted, so that verse 30 of M would make no sense if it had been literally
translated by G. G therefore renders פדה נפשי (vs. 28) 'he redeemed my
soul' as ἀλλ' ἐρρύσατο τὴν ψυχήν μου (ἐκ θανάτου representing מני־שחת of vs.
30). חיתי באור תראה of M verse 28 is treated as ἵνα ἡ ζωή μου ἐν φωτὶ αἰνῇ
αὐτόν; 'in order that my life in light may praise him' in G verse 30. תראה
'it may see' of M verse 28, by reading ר for ד, is treated as if it were from
the Hiphil of the root ירה 'praise' and translated as αἰνῇ 'praise'. The

---

[1]Cf., supra, p. 56.

ל of לאור in verse 30 is rendered as ἵνα in line 2 of G verse 30. By treating

the Hebrew in this way the translator eliminates the concept that God plays

with man (vs. 29) and also the inconsistency of the Hebrew (vs. 22 as compared

with vs. 30). In G the reason that Elihu is redeemed by God is that he may

praise God. G thus contrasts the life of the wicked with that of Elihu:

'And his soul drew near unto death;   ἤγγισεν δὲ εἰς θάνατον ἡ ψυχὴ αὐτοῦ,
And his life is in Hades.'   ἡ δὲ ζωὴ αὐτοῦ ἐν ᾅδῃ.
But he redeemed my soul from death   ἀλλ' ἐρρύσατο τὴν ψυχήν μου ἐκ θανάτου,
In order that my life in light may   ἵνα ἡ ζωή μου ἐν φωτὶ αἰνῇ αὐτόν.
  praise him.'

   Elihu in chapter 35 presents a rather confused recapitulation of

his accusations against Job. In the course of this argument he appeals to the

transcendence of God which places God beyond receiving either injury or aid

from human beings. Addressing his rhetorical questions to Job Elihu asks

(M 35:6):

  'If thou hast sinned, what achievest thou   אם־חטאת מה־תפעל־בו
    against him?
  And if thy transgressions be many, what do-   ורבו פשעיך מה־תעשה־לו
    est thou unto him?'

By omitting בו and לו which refer to God G removes the suggestion in the He-

brew text that one could do anything against God. G thus presents the fu-

tility of the one who sins:

'If thou hast sinned, what wilt thou   εἰ ἥμαρτες, τί πράξεις;
    achieve?
And if thou hast committed many trans-   εἰ δὲ καὶ πολλὰ ἠνόμησας, τί δύνασαι
  gressions, what art thou able to do?'   ποιῆσαι;

   The examples cited above prove that the Greek translator avoids

or changes descriptions in the Hebrew text which cast reflections upon the

perfect character of God or could by misinterpretation be so understood.

   The translator further eschews any portrayal of God as the agent

of destruction or persecution of man, since such an expression would not

appear commendatory to God. The second division of this chapter, therefore, deals with the following theme:

Portrayals of God as the Agent of Destruction

or the Persecutor of Man Avoided

or Changed by the Translator

The scene for Job's sufferings is set in the introductory prose
section to the Book of Job. While Job's sons and daughters are banqueting,
a messenger comes to Job to announce that his oxen and asses together with the
men who tend them have been attacked by the hosts of Sheba. While this messenger is finishing his dire tidings, another comes with the news that Job's
sheep and goats have been consumed by lightning. The messenger says (M 1:16):[1]

'The fire of God fell from heaven.' אֵשׁ אלהים נפלה מן דשׁמים

The translator understands אֵשׁ אלהים as signifying lightning, but he removes
any possible interpretation of the words as denoting destructive action on the
part of God by omitting אלהים and reading:

'Fire fell from heaven.'[2] Πῦρ ἔπεσεν ἐκ τοῦ οὐρανοῦ

By way of contrast to the above example in which G avoids linking
the name of God with destruction or deception there should be noted the fact
that G does not rewrite the Hebrew text in every such instance. He attempts to
leave evidences of the Hebrew *Vorlage*, while following a method of evaluating
the degree of aversion which he experiences in treating passages of the Hebrew
text. In chapters 4 and 5 Eliphaz, after 'having remained silent for a week
in deference to the sufferings of Job, begins to exhort Job to have confidence
in the fear of God. Eliphaz describes a vision in which he hears a voice pro-

----

[1]Cf., Gehman, *op. cit.*, p. 235; Gerleman, *op. cit.*, p. 58.

[2]For a discussion of 2:3, cf., Gehman, *op. cit.*, pp. 231-32.

claiming that no mortal can be considered as just before God, since God ascribes error even to his angels (M 4:18b):

'And his angels he chargeth with error.' וּבְמַלְאָכָיו יָשִׂים תָּהֳלָה

Here the translator apparently takes no offense that God performs such action.
The reason may be that in this line God is not depicted either as destroying or
misleading, but merely points out error which already exists. G reads:

'And he conceives (contrives, intends) a   κατὰ δὲ ἀγγέλων αὐτοῦ σκολιόν τι
   certain crookedness against his angels.'   ἐπενόησεν.

When Bildad addresses Job, he insists that God does not reject a
perfect man or accept a wicked one. Job replies (chaps. 9-10) that he knows
that if a man wished to contend with God for the purpose of establishing his
own righteousness, he would be doomed to failure. Job expounds the power of
God as he declares (M 9:12a):

'If he seizeth, who can turn him back?' הֵן יַחְתֹּף מִי יְשִׁיבֶנּוּ

In avoiding the undignified picture of God implied in הֵן יַחְתֹּף, G renders the
words freely as ἐὰν ἀπαλλάξῃ 'if he set free':

'If he set free, who will turn (him) back?' ἐὰν ἀπαλλάξῃ, τίς ἀποστρέψει;

Then Job draws a contrast of man to God. In verse 12 man is depicted as
unable to turn back God's anger. In the following verse God, who might turn
his own anger back, does not (M 9:13):

'God doth not turn back his anger.' אֱלוֹהַּ לֹא־יָשִׁיב אַפּוֹ

Job's thought is that man is exposed to this anger if he happens to be in the
way. In other words, the anger of God is tremendous force, inanimate and irresistible. The translator does not like this rather mechanical idea of the work-
ings of God, and so he omits the suffix וֹ from אַפּוֹ and the negative לֹא and renders:

'For he himself has turned back anger.' αὐτὸς γὰρ ἀπέστραπται ὀργήν.

In this way G depicts the anger of God as tempered by his mercy.

Sophar in chapter 11 merely reiterates what Bildad (8:5-7, 20-22)
and Eliphaz (5:17ff.) had previously stated. Job should purge himself of iniquity and return to God so that all will be well with him. Job answers
(chaps. 12-14)[1] that God's action disproves such a platitude. After he appeals
to his companions to allow him the opportunity of speaking, Job petitions
God for a fair trial. He asks God to make known the iniquities and sins with
which he may be charged. Receiving no reply to this Job suggests by a series
of questions that God is too severe and capricious in his treatment of man.

Eliphaz, therefore, feels himself called upon to speak a second time
(chap. 15) in rebuttal to Job. He condemns Job for his irreverence and pro-
nounces certain doom upon the godless. Job dismisses such charges as being the
product of unsympathetic observation of the true nature of his afflications.
Job describes God's violent treatment of him in M 16:13-14:

'His archers compass me round about;   יסבו עלי רביו
He cleaveth through my reins and doth not spare; יפלח כליותי ולא יחמול
He poureth out my gall upon the ground;   ישפך לארץ מררתי
He breaketh me with breach upon breach;   יפרצני פרץ על־פני־פרץ
He runneth upon me like a warrior.'   ירץ עלי כנבור

The translator removes God from the passage by changing the number of the verbs
from the singular to the plural indefinite. In M God slays Job; in G, indefinite enemies or troubles kill him. G reads:

'They surrounded me with lances;   ἐκύκλωσάν με λόγχαις
Having thrown into my kidneys (and) not sparing, βάλλοντες εἰς νεφρούς μου οὐ φειδό-
They poured out my gall upon the ground; μενοι, ἐξέχεαν εἰς τὴν γῆν τὴν χολήν μου·
They cast me down, misfortune upon misfortune; κατέβαλόν με πτῶμα ἐπὶ πτώματι,
They ran against me, being powerful.'   ἔδραμον πρός με δυνάμενοι.

When Job replies to Bildad's accusations in chapter 18, he asks

---

[1]Cf., Gehman, *op. cit.*, p. 235, for a discussion of 13:15.

(chap. 19) how long the friends will accuse him so unjustly. He insists that

his present state is the result only of God's unjust and violent treatment of

him (M 19:6a):

'Know then that God hath subverted me.' דעו־אפו כי־אלוה עותני

The root עות in the Piel has the idea of 'make crooked, falsify, pervert' and

therefore deprive of justice'. The translator omits the suffix נ־י from the

verb and renders:

'Know thereforee that the Lord is he who γνῶτε οὖν ὅτι ὁ κύριός ἐστιν ὁ
    has troubled (disturbed).'   ταράξας.

The idea that Job accuses God of depriving him of justice is thereby eliminated.

In Job's reply (chap. 24) to the third speech of Eliphaz he describes

those who transgress the commandments of God: the murderer, thief, and adul-

terer (M 24:14-19):

'The murdeer riseth with the light to kill the poor and needy;	לאור יקום רוצח יקטל־עני ואביון
And in the night he is also a thief.	ובלילה יהי כגנב
The eye also of the adulterer waiteth for the twilight,	ועין נאף שמרה נשף
Saying: No eye shall see me;	לאמר לא־תשורני עין
And he putteth a covering on his face.	וסתר פנים ישים
In the dark they dig through houses;	חתר בחשך בתים
They shut themselves up in the day-time;	יומם חתמו־למו
They know not the light.	לא־ידעו אור
For the deep gloom is to all of them as the morn-ing;	כי יחדו בקר למו צלמות
For they know the terrors of the deep gloom.	כי־יכיר בלהות צלמות
He (God) is swift upon the face of the waters;	קל־הוא על־פני־מים
Their portion is cursed in the earth;	תקלל חלקתם בארץ
He turneth not by the way of the vineyards.	לא־יפנה דרך כרמים
Crought and heat consume the snow waters;	ציה גם־חם יגזלו מימי־שלג
So doth Sheol those that have sinned.'	שאול חטאו

The translator omits verses 14b-18 to avoid the minutiae of criminal action which

are described. In 18bc of the Hebrew God is depicted as chastening the wicked,

and verse 19 shows the certain punishment of sinners. In light of the context

(vss. 18-24), such a penalty would seem arbitrary and would denote a severe

treatment of some transgressors and a lenient one of others without apparent

moral discrimination. G therefore rewrites the Hebrew text of 14a, 18bc, and
19. In verse 18b the translator renders the Hebrew text accurately, although
he expresses a wish instead of an indicative statement. G omits לא־יפנה דרך
of verse 18c, but freely renders כרמים as τὰ φυτά 'the plants' and placés it
into line 1 of verse 19. G then freely translates ציה of line 1 in verse 19
as ἐπὶ γῆς ξηρά dry upon the earth' and the root גזל in line 1 as ἀρπάζω
'snatch away' which is placed into line 2 of verse 19. חם of line 1 in verse
10 suggests יתום 'orphan', which G renders as ὀρφανοί 'orphans' in line 2 of
verse 19. The translator thus makes a good sequence of thought which depicts
the doom of the wicked. G reads:

'And having known their deeds he (God) γνοὺς δὲ αὐτῶν τὰ ἔργα παρέδωκεν
 delivered them into darkness. αὐτοὺς εἰς σκότος,
May their portion be cursed upon the earth,καταραθείη ἡ μερὶς αὐτῶν ἐπὶ γῆς.
And may their plants appear dry upon the ἀναφανείη δὲ τὰ φυτὰ αὐτῶν ἐπὶ
 earth! γῆς ξηρά·
For they snatched away the arms of orphans.' ἀγκαλίδα γὰρ ὀρφανῶν ἥρπασαν.

  When Elihu repeats the arguments of his friends (chaps. 32-37), he
describes the activity of God. He maintains that God who is omniscient never
fails to observe and punish sin. Elihu thus delineates God's treatment of the
wicked (M 34:24-26):

'He breaketh in pieces mighty men without investigation,ירע כבירים לא־חקר
And setteth others in their stead. ויעמד אחרים תחתם
Therefore, he taketh knowledge of their works; לכן יכיר מעבדיהם
And he overturneth (them) in the night so that they are והפך לילה וידכאו
 crushed.
He striketh them as wicked men תחת־רשעים ספקם
In the open sight of others.' במקום ראים

Verse 24 of the Hebrew presents the greatness of God in the field of destruction. The Hebrew means that God need not investigate men, since he already
knows all things. By rewriting ירע כבירים of line 1 and interpreting as
ὁ καταλαμβάνων 'he who takes hold of', and by rendering לא־חקר of line 1
as ἀνεξιχνίαστα 'inscrutable things', the translator portrays God's control

of hidden things. G then rewrites line 2 to expand upon God's performance of

marvellous things. In verse 25 G drops לָב and makes the first line describe

God who makes known the deeds of the ἀσεβεῖς in verse 26. The translator omits

line 2 of verse 25 because it again seems to depict the omnipotence of God

only with reference to destruction. He then tones down the first line of verse

26 somewhat by rendering מָקֵפ as ἔσβεσεν 'he quenched, put out', with the sub-

ject ὁ γνωρίζων 'he who makes known' taken from verse 25a. Both the Hebrew

and Greek texts, however, mean that God destroyed the wicked. At any rate,

the constructive might of God is stressed by G more than by M. G reads:

'He who takes hold of inscrutable things,   ὁ καταλαμβάνων ἀνεξιχνίαστα,
Marvellous and extraordinary things which   ἔνδοξά τε καὶ ἐξαίσια, ὧν οὐκ
   are without number;   ἔστιν ἀριθμός·
He who makes known their (the ungodly's)   ὁ γνωρίζων αὐτῶν τὰ ἔργα
   deeds,
Moreover quelled the wicked,   ἔσβεσεν δὲ ἀσεβεῖς,
While there were lookers-on before him (God).' ὁρατοὶ δὲ ἐναντίον αὐτοῦ.

In the last section of his speech (chaps. 36-37) Elihu upholds the

idea that God treats a man according to his works. Suffering, Elihu contends,

is merely discipline from God. Thus it is that Elihu declares (M 36:15):

'He delivereth the wronged by the wrong which he (man) suffers יְחַלֵּץ עָנִי בְעָנְיוֹ
And openeth their ear by means of distress.'   וְיִגֶל בַּלַּחַץ אָזְנָם

The translator wishes to avoid the idea that God would wrong anyone even if for

disciplinary reasons. He therefore rewrites the first line of the Hebrew and

applies it to the ungodly (mentioned in vs. 12 of G), who oppress the helpless.

He further eliminates the concept in line 2 that God opens the ear of the wrong-

ed through distress. Instead G portrays the judgment of God as being in favour

of the meek.   G reads:

'Because they (the wicked) afflicted the ἀνθ᾽ ὧν ἔθλιψαν ἀσθενῆ καὶ ἀδύνατον·
   weak and powerless,
He (God) will exhibit judgment (in favour) κρίμα δὲ πραέων ἐκθήσει.
   of the meek.'

It is Elihu's contention that for an ignorant human being to present his case before God is to ask for destruction. Elihu has no desire to
do so, for he says (M 37:20):

'Should it be told[1]him that I would speak?   היספר־לו כי אדבר
Or does a man speak when he will be swallowed up?[2]' אם־אמר איש כי יבלע

The translator avoids the idea of man talking to God, by employing in line 1
a doublet of היספר; this is read as ספר and rendered first as βίβλος 'book'
then as γραμματεύς 'scribe'. He then reads לו as לי 'to me' and makes thereby a transfer from speaking to God to addressing man. M implies in line 2
that God does not give man a chance. G apparently does not like the suggestion
that God would swallow up or destroy an innocent man. אמר in line 2 may have
suggested עמד 'stand', for G translates as ἑστηκώς 'standing up'. G thus produces the sense that Elihu has no help (a book or scribe to prompt him) to silence a man:

'There has not stood beside me, has there, μὴ βίβλος ἢ γραμματεύς μοι παρέστηκεν,
    a book or a scribe,
In order that I, standing up, may silence ἵνα ἄνθρωπον ἑστηκὼς κατασιωπήσω;
    a man?'

After Elihu has described the might and strength of God, he marvels
at the incomprehensible nature of the Almighty. For this reason Elihu declares (M 37:24):

'Men do therefore fear him;   לכן יראוהו אנשים
He regardeth not any that are wise of heart.' לא־יראה כל־חכמי־לב

G avoids any possible interpretation of M that God would not regard or see things.
The Hebrew text cannot mean that God is blind. It must mean that God merely does

----

[1]Ehrlich, op. cit., p. 235, calls יספר the Pual of ספר which has
'clouds' as its subject and means 'dispersed' or 'scattered' here. He says to
compare Arabic ﺳﻔﺮ . . . das ebenfalls mit Bezug auf Gewoelk so gebraucht
wird'. He suggests that לו, depending upon a mistaken interpretation of the
meaning of יספר, be omitted.

[2]Duhm, op. cit., ad. loc., reads as if from the root בלל 'confuse'

not consider the wise of heart. Such an idea appears to the translator to re-
flect injustice on the part of God. G therefore plays with לא in line 2, reading it as לו 'him'. יראה is treated as plural in number from the root ירא
'fear' and rendered as φοβηθήσονται 'they fear', with the wise in heart as subject. G reads:

'Therefore men will fear him --   διὸ φοβηθήσονται αὐτὸν οἱ ἄνθρωποι,
Yea, the wise of heart do fear him.' φοβηθήσονται δὲ αὐτὸν καὶ οἱ σοφοὶ καρδίᾳ.

Yahweh now speaks to Job out of the tempest (chaps. 38-41). After
proclaiming the transcendence of his own ways and the marvels of his creation
(chaps. 38-39) God describes the great beasts Behemoth and Leviathan. Concerning Behemoth (chap. 40) God says (M 40:19):

'He is the beginning of the ways of God: הוא ראשית דרכי־אל
Let him that made him bring near his sword.'   העשו יגש חרבו

The second line of the Hebrew text presents God as destroying his own creation.
It also portrays God as wielding a sword. G changes these descriptions of God
by the following method. Line 1 of M is translated freely to avoid the ab-
straction of the Hebrew text. In line 2 G interprets the participle העשו, by
attaching י through dittography from the following word, as a passive העשוי
'Having been made'. Metathesis is employed with חרבו to produce חבריו 'his
(God's) companions' which is then translated as τῶν ἀγγέλων αὐτοῦ 'his angels'.
The meaning of the root נגש in יגש is interpreted in the sense of 'approach in
order to play with'. G accordingly renders:

'This is the first of that fashioned   τοῦτ' ἔστιν ἀρχὴ πλάσματος κυρίου,
    by God,
Having been made to be played with by   πεποιημένον ἐγκαταπαίζεσθαι ὑπὸ τῶν
    his angels.'   ἀγγέλων αὐτοῦ.

In this connection there must be noted a similar translation by G of the Hebrew.
In chapter 41 God describes the strength and might of Leviathan, concerning
whom he says (M 41:25):

'Upon earth there is not his like –:– אֵין־עַל־עָפָר מָשְׁלוֹ
Which is made without fear.' הֶעָשׂוּ לִבְלִי־חָת

The second line means that the beast is fearless. The translator, however,

connects Leviathan with Behemoth by quoting his rendering of M 40:19. In

addition he exalts the angels by stating that they are not afraid to play

with Leviathan. G reads:

'For there is nothing like him upon   οὐκ ἔστιν οὐδὲν ἐπὶ τῆς γῆς ὅμοιον
      the earth --   αὐτῷ
Having been made to be played with   πεποιημένον ἐγκαταπαίζεσθαι ὑπὸ τῶν
      by mine angels.'   ἀγγέλων μου·

Job now gives up his argument against God by repudiating his statements and by

repenting in dust and ashes (42:6). In the prose epilogue which follows (42:7-

17) all the relatives and friends of Job who knew him in the days of prosperity

come in unto him and offer their sympathy (M 42:11b):

'. . . and they showed their grief for him, and comforted   וַיָּנֻדוּ לוֹ וַיְנַחֲמוּ אֹתוֹ
him for   the evil which Yahweh had brought upon him.'עַל כָּל־הָרָעָה אֲשֶׁר־הֵבִיא יְהוָה עָלָיו

The   translator avoids saying that God had brought evil upon Job by omitting

הָרָעָה and by interpreting יְנַחֲמוּ in the sense of 'being amazed'. G reads:

'. . . they comforted him and they   παρεκάλεσαν αὐτόν, καὶ ἐθαύμασαν ἐπὶ
were amazed at all those things which   πᾶσιν, οἷς ἐπήγαγεν αὐτῷ ὁ κύριος·
the Lord had brought   to him.'

The examples cited in this chapter prove that the translator does

not set out to   rewrite the Hebrew text. He rather follows a method of inter-

pretation which avoids casting any reflection upon the moral character of God.

He is not bound by any clearly prescribed system of rendering, but rather is

free to evaluate the theological significance of a passage in question and

then to stress some phases of the thought and to soften others. He does, how-

ever, tend to eliminate derogatory descriptions of God and to lessen the force

of destructive action wrought by the Almighty as presented in the *Vorlage*.

The result of this tendency is a Greek text which often appears to differ radically from the Hebrew. The fact is, however, that the Hebrew upon which G is founded can in almost every instance be visualized and be shown to be very similar to the text of M. An understanding, therefore, of the method by which any disparagement of the character of God is avoided by the translator is essential   for a careful study of the Greek version of the Book of Job.

CHAPTER IV

THEOLOGICAL OMISSIONS FROM

THE GREEK TEXT

Mention occasionally has been made in the preceding chapters of passages of the Hebrew text which G omits for theological reasons. In this chapter there are discussed other passages which are omitted from the Greek text in accordance with the translator's theological approach to exegesis.

It is clear from the evidence presented in the earlier part of this study that G worked with a Hebrew text, the *Vorlage*, which is very similar to M. There are, however, many lines of the Hebrew text of Job which are not represented by the translator. When Origen compiled the Hexapla, he evolved a system of denoting such lacunae in the Old Greek text. Whenever he found words or expressions in the Hebrew which were lacking in the Greek text, he supplied them from the translations of the Three or from the Hebrew, and indicated the beginning of the addition with an asterisk and its conclusion with a metobelus.[1] The Septuagint version of Job, of which Codex Vaticanus exhibits a text relatively closest to the original Old Greek text, appears therefore to be far shorter than M. For reasons, however, which will be presented in this chapter, the writer upholds the proposition that G and M both represent substantially the same *Vorlage*.

The first group of passages omitted by the translator are those which may be grouped under the following theme:

----

[1]Rahlfs, *op. cit.*, attempts to preserve these markings in his Greek text of Job.

Theological Toning Down

Just as the translator tones down passages which offend him, so he also omits other passages in order theologically to soften statements in the Hebrew text..

Chapters 9 and 10 show Job's taking up Bildad's conception of divine might and justice. He recognizes the irresistible power of God and the fact that, if God insists on condemning him as guilty, then Job cannot establish his own innocence. Yet Job maintains that Bildad is wrong in saying that God shows discrimination in exercising might and justice, for innocent and guilty alike seem to be subject to the moral indifference of God. Job says (M 9:22-25):

'It is (all) one -- therefore I say,	אחת היא על־כן אמרתי
The innocent and the wicked he bringeth to an end.	תם ורשע הוא מכלה.
If the scourge slay suddenly,	אם־שוט ימית פתאם
At the trial of the guiltless he will mock.	למסת נקים ילעג
The earth is given into the hand of the wicked;	ארץ נתנה ביד־רשע
He covereth the faces of the judges thereof;	פני־שפטיה יכסה.
If (it be) not (God) then, who then is it?	אם־לא אפוא מי־הוא
Now my days are swifter than a runner;	וימי קלו מני־רץ
They flee away, they see no good.'	ברחו לא־ראו טובה

The Greek treatment of 9:20-23 has already been discussed by Gehman.[1] The translator removes God from verse 23 and introduces the δίκαιοι 'just' into line 2. In verse 24 G tones down the idea that the earth is given over to wicked men, by continuing δίκαιοι as subject of the verb in line 1. Lines 2 and 3 of verse 24 are omitted to avoid the concept that God would cover up the eyes of judges. G then treats 'מי in line 1 of verse 25 as ὁ βίος μου 'my life' and omits שובה in line 2. G accordingly renders:

'Therefore I said, A mighty one and a ruler	διὸ εἶπον Μέγαν καὶ δυνάστην
wrath destroys	ἀπολλύει ὀργή.

---

[1]*Op. cit.*, p. 234.

Because the evil (are) in a violent death;	ὅτι φαῦλοι ἐν θανάτῳ ἐξαισίῳ,
But the just are laughed to scorn,	ἀλλὰ δίκαιοι καταγελῶνται·
For they have been given over into the hands	παραδέδονται γὰρ εἰς χεῖρας ἀσεβοῦς.
of an ungodly one.	
But my life is swifter than a runner:	ὁ δὲ βίος μου ἐστιν ἐλαφρότερος δρομέως·
They fled away and did not see.'[1]	ἀπέδρασαν καὶ οὐκ εἴδοσαν.

In his second speech (chap. 15) Eliphaz suggests that Job's wickedness exceeds even the universality of human unrighteousness (15:14-16). In this connection Eliphaz describes the conduct of the wicked man who behaves himself proudly even against God (M 15:26-28a):

'He runneth upon him (God) with a stiff neck,[2]	ירוץ אליו בצואר
With the thick buckles of his shield;	בעבי גבי מגניו
Because he hath covered his face with his fatness	כי־כסה פניו בחלבו
And made collops of fat on his loins;	ויעש פימה עלי־כסל
And he hath dwelt in desolate cities.'	וישכון ערים נכחדות

The translator avoids the offensive picture of man's being able to confirm his insensibility to God through fatness by omitting verses 26b and 27. G then expresses the doom which it is hoped will befall such an one, by recasting 28a as a wish:

'But he ran before him with insolence;	ἔδραμεν δὲ ἐναντίον αὐτοῦ ὕβρει
But may he inhabit deserted cities.'	αὐλισθείη δὲ πόλεις ἐρήμους.

Sophar (chap. 20) tells Job that the wicked most certainly will receive the punishment which is their due. Job, however, cites facts (chap. 21) to prove that Sophar's contention is false. Job states that the wicked openly defy God with impunity (M 21:14-16):

'Yet they (the wicked) said unto God, Depart from us;	ויאמרו לאל סור ממנו
For we desire not the knowledge of thy ways.	ודעת דרכיך לא חפצנו
What is the Almighty, that we should serve him?	מה־שדי כי נעבדנו
And what profit would we have, if we pray unto him?	ומה־נועיל כי נפגע־בו
Lo, their prosperity is not in their hand.	הן לא בידם טובם
The counsel of the wicked is far from me.'	עצת רשעים רחקה מני

---

[1] Apparently the translator disregarded the fact that he had translated ימי in l. 1 of vs. 25 as ὁ βίος μου, and retained the plural in the second line of the verse. Although βίος is introduced in l. 1, 'days' (understood) would be in parallelism to it and must be considered as the subject in l. 2.

[2] Cf., Gehman, op. cit., p. 239, for a toning down of אל by ἐναντίον.

In his attempt to interpret the Hebrew text the translator renders verse 14
with a change from the plural to the singular number to show that the wickedness is of one transgressor instead of many. Verse 15, however, is considered as   too blasphemous a statement with reference to the Almighty. The translator therefore omits the verse entirely. The Hebrew of verse 16a indicates
that Job apparently recognizes that the prosperity of the wicked is not theirs
to retain but must be secured to them by God. G omits לא in verse 16a, thereby retaining the idea of verse 13 that the wicked complete their days in prosperity. In verse 16b the translator apparently played with מני, reading it as
ממנו 'from him (God). The reason may be that he desires to show that God does
not watch over the deeds of the wicked in the sense of conducting their activities. The question may also be asked, Is the final י of מני an abbrevia-
tion for יהוה? If G understood מני in this sense then its rendering of the
Hebrew indicates that the subject of ἐφορᾷ is God. At any rate, it seems G
read מני as ממנו and therefore reads:

'But he saith to the Lord, Depart from me,	λέγει δὲ κυρίῳ Ἀπόστα ἀπ' ἐμοῦ,
For I do not desire to know thy ways.	ὁδούς σου εἰδέναι οὐ βούλομαι·
For in (their) hands was their prosperity,	ἐν χερσὶν γὰρ ἦν αὐτῶν τὰ ἀγαθά,
But he doth not watch over the deeds of the wicked.'	ἔργα δὲ ἀσεβῶν οὐκ ἐφορᾷ.

In the independent poem (chap. 28) wisdom is described as being
beyond the abilityy of man to understand. Wisdom is portrayed as so priceless
that it is impossible for a man to acquire it at any price. In M 28:13-23 M
reads:

'Man knoweth not the price of it;	לא־ידע אנוש ערכה
Neither is it found in the land of the living.	ולא תמצא בארץ החיים
The deep saith, It is not in me:	תהום אמר לא בי־היא
And the sea saith, It is not with me.	וים אמר אין עמדי
It cannot be gotten for gold;	לא־יתן סגור תחתיה
Neither can silver be weighed as the price of it.	ולא ישקל כסף מחירה
It cannot be valued with the gold of Ophir	לא־תסלה בכתם אופיר
With the precious onyx or the sapphire.	בשהם יקר וספיר
Gold and glass cannot equal it;	לא־יערכנה זהב וזכוכית

Neither can the exchange thereof be vessels of ותמורתה כלי-פז
    fine gold.
No mention can be made of coral or crystal; ראמות וגביש לא יזכר
Yea, the price of wisdom is above pearls. ומשך חכמה מפנינים
The topaz of Ethiopia doth not equal it; לא-יערכנה פטדת-כוש
Neither can it be valued with pure gold. בכתם שהור לא תסלה
Whence then cometh wisdom? והחכמה מאין בוא
And where is the place of understanding? ואי זה מקום בינה
Seeing it is hid from the eyes of all living, ונעלמה מעיני כל-חי
And kept close from the fowls of the air. ומעוף השמים נסתרה
Abaddon and death say, אבדון ומות אמרו
We have heard a rumour thereof with our ears. באזנינו שמענו שמעה
God understandeth the way to it, אלהים הבין דרכה
And he knoweth the place thereof.' והוא ידע את-מקומה

G is more matter-of-fact than is the Hebrew text in its rendering, and the
omission of verses 14-19 does not injure the sequence of thought in the chapter. The main reason, however, why the translator omits verses 14-19 is two-
fold: (1) to avoid the possible mythological reference to Tiamat in 14a
(צהום); and (2) to avoid the personification of the deep and the sea. G o-
mits verses 21b and 22a to avoid the concept that the fowls of the air could
possibly be considered as possessing wisdom or that 'Abaddon' and 'death'
could be personified in a mythological sense. G accordingly presents the in-
attainability of wisdom by rendering:

'A mortal does not know the way of it, οὐκ οἶδεν βροτὸς ὁδὸν αὐτῆς,
Nor will it be found among men. οὐδὲ μὴ εὑρεθῇ ἐν ἀνθρώποις.
But as for wisdom, whence was it found? ἡ δὲ σοφία πόθεν εὑρέθη;
But what sort of place belongeth to under- ποῖος δὲ τόπος ἐστὶν τῆς συνέως;
    standing?
It has escaped the notice of every man; λέληθεν πάντα ἄνθρωπον
But we have heard the fame thereof.' Ἀκηκόαμεν δὲ αὐτῆς τὸ κλέος.

      In chapter 35 Elihu extols the transcendence of God which sets God
apart from any effect which the acts of men produce. Job had already admitted
(7:20) the fact that neither good nor evil deeds of men could in any way injure or benefit God. Elihu, nevertheless, declares to Job (M 35:7-10):

'If thou be righteous, what givest thou to him (God)? אם-צדקת מה-תתן-לו
Or what doth he receive from thy hand? או מה-מידך יקח
And thy wickedness concerns a man like thyself, לאיש-כמוך רשעך
And an ordinary man, thy righteousness. ולבן-אדם צדקתך

By reason of the multitude of oppressions, they cry out; מרב עשוקים יזעיקו
They cry for help by reason of the arm of the mighty. ישועו מזרוע רבים
But none said, Where is God my Maker ולא־אמר איה אלוה עשי
Who giveth songs in the night?' נתן זמרות בלילה

The translator objects to the anthropomorphic concept of God in verse 7b which implies that God would reach out to take something from the hand of man, and so he omits the line. G enhances the character of Job whenever possible. It therefore omits verse 8a.which ascribes wickedness to Job. Verses 8b, 9, and 10 in the Hebrew text thus would make no sense in the context of G, and so the translator omits verses 8b, 9, and 10a. שם of verse 10b suggests שמר 'keep' or 'watch', which G translates as φυλακάς 'guards, watches'. These 'night watches' probably refer to God's handiwork in heaven, such as the stars, the moon, or the constellations. 'Ο κατατάσσων 'he who establisheth' of verse 10b thus makes a logical, though not grammatical transition from αὐτῷ 'to him' in verse 7a. The participle ὁ κατατάσσων would be dative in agreement with αὐτῷ, if the translator's *Vorlage* had been lacking in verses 7b-10a. The nominative here shows that he translated literally and forgot to place ὁ κατατάσσων in agreement with αὐτῷ. The grammatical discrepancy proves that the translator was working with a long text, not with a shorter one. G accordingly renders:

'But since then thou art righteous, what ἐπεὶ δὲ οὖν δίκαιος εἶ, τί δώσεις
    wilt thou give to him?   αὐτῷ;
(It is) he who establisheth night watches.'ὁ κατατάσσων φυλακὰς νυκτερινάς.

In addition to omitting certain passages from the Hebrew *Vorlage* for the reason sdiscussed above, the translator also leaves out verses or lines which detract from an elevated concept of God:

Disparagement of the Perfect
Character of God Avoided

When Job (chaps. 6-7) replies to the first speech of Eliphaz, he addresses the last part of his remarks directly to God (7:7-21). In his lone-

liness Job cries out to God, saying (M 7:7-9):

'O, remember that my life is wind; זכר כי־רוח חיי
Mine eye will no more see good. לא־תשוב עיני לראות טוב
The eye of him (God) that seeth me will behold me לא־תשורני עין ראי
  no more.
Thine (God's) eyes will be upon me, but I shall עיניך בי ואינני
  not be.
A cloud cometh to an end and vanisheth away; כלה ענן וילך
So he that goeth down to Sheol cometh up no more.' כן יורד שאול לא יעלה

The translator omits verse 8, thereby avoiding the inference that God is limit-

ed and cannot see Job at all times. By this omission verses 7 and 9 are drawn

together to form a good transition of thought. G renders the first line of

verse 9 freely and reads:

'Remember then that my life is breath; μνήσθητι οὖν ὅτι πνεῦμά μου ἡ ζωὴ
And mine eye will no longer rise up to see good, καὶ οὐκέτι ἐπανελεύσεται ὁ ὀφθαλμός
As a cloud swept clean from heaven. μου ἰδεῖν ἀγαθόν. ὥσπερ νέφος ἀποκαθαρθὲν ἀπ' οὐ-
For if a man descend into Hades, he will not again ρανοῦ. ἐὰν γὰρ ἄνθρωπος καταβῇ
  ascend.' εἰς ᾅδην, οὐκέτι μὴ ἀναβῇ.

        Sophar repeats in chapter 11 the platitudes of Bildad (8:5-7, 20-22) and

of Eliphaz (5:17ff.) concerning Job's course of action. Sophar exhorts Job to

purge himself of wickedness and to return to the Almighty so that all may be well.

Job replies (chaps. 12-14) that Sophar's platitudes are proved false by God's

action. Job maintains that God through his own desires leads astray nations and

their leaders. Concerning this activity of God Job says (M 12:22-23):

'Who (God) discovereth deep things out of darkness, מגלה עמקות מני־חשך
And bringeth out to light deep gloom; ויצא לאור צלמות
Who increaseth nations and destroyeth them; משגיא לגוים ויאבדם
Who enlargeth the nations and leadeth them away.' שטח לגוים וינחם

The translator objects to the idea in line 1 of verse 23 that God destroys

nations. He therefore omits the line. In line 2 of verse 22 G employs a

literalism, reading צלמות as two words צל מות 'shadow of death', which he trans-

lates exactly as σκία θανάτου. Line 2 of verse 23 is rendered freely according

to context and G reads:

'He -- revealing deep things out of shadow,   ἀνακαλύπτων βαθέα ἐκ σκότους,
Led out into the light (the) shadow of   ἐξήγαγεν δὲ εἰς φῶς σκιὰν θανάτου.
    death,
Spreading out nations and leading them away.'κατασ}ρωννύων ἔθνη καὶ καθοδηγῶν
                                              αὐτά.

Job admits (chap. 13) that he has from personal experience seen and

understood that punishment is inevitable for the wicked. Job, however, is con-

viaced of his own innocence of any sin which would call the wrath of God

upon him. He therefore appeals directly to God, asking (M 13:20):

'Only two things do not unto me,   אך־שתים אל־תעש עמדי
Then will I not hide myself from thy face,'   אז מפניך לא אסתר

By omitting the negative אל from line 1 the translator avoids the idea that Job

could command God not to do anything toc him. He then renders תעש freely by

χρήσῃ 'use, treat, deal with', thereby portraying Job as praying to God how to

treat him. G eliminates the possibility that Job could hide himself from God,

and it also removes the anthropomorphic expression מפניך by leaving out line 2

entirely. Thus goes G:

        'But in two ways deal thou with me.' δυεῖν δέ μοι χρήσῃ·

In chapter 14 Job feels himself to be hopelessly condemned. He de-

clares that his transgressions are sealed up for the day of reckoning (M 14:

17-20a):

'And thou hast plastered (glued) over mine iniquity.   ותטפל על־עוני
But indeed a mountain falling, crumbleth away,   ואולם הר־נופל יבול
And a rock is removed out of its place;   וצור יעתק ממקמו
The waters wear the stones;   אבנים שחקו מים
The overflowings thereof wash away the dust of the   תשטף־ספיחיה עפר־ארץ
    earth:
And thou destroyest the hope of man.   ותקות אנוש האבדת
Thou prevailest forever against him, and he passeth   תתקפהו לנצח ויהלך
    away.'

The treatment of verse 17b has already been discussed by Gehman.[1] G objects to

----

[1]Op. cit., pp. 237-38.

the idea in verses 18 and 19 that God destroys the hope of man by constantly
wearing him down like the erosion of a mountain or a rock; so it omits these
lines. G does not rewrite the Hebrew text entirely, however, for it retains
verse 20a and reads:

'But thou didst put on thy seal if I un-   ἐπεσημήνω δέ, εἴ τι ἄκων παρέβην.
   wittingly committed any transgression;
Thou didst drive him to the limit and he ὦσας αὐτὸν εἰς τέλος, καὶ ᾤχετο·
   perished.'

     Sophar insists in chapter 20 that any prosperity the wicked may
enjoy is ephemeral. He declares that the ultimate fate of evil-doers is
the loss of everything that they cherish. Job (chap. 21) cannot believe such
truisms concerning the doom of the transgressors. He quotes the impertinent
words of the wicked who tell God to depart from them and who declare that
prayer is of no profit to them. Job then quotes Eliphaz and Sophar as having
said (M 21:19a):

'God layeth up his (the wicked's) iniquity for   אלוה יצפן־לבניו אונו
    his children.'

Because G objects to the doctrine of transmitted guilt, he renders the verse as
follows:[1]

'Let his (the wicked's) possessions fail   .ἐκλίποι υἱοὺς τὰ ὑπάρχοντα αὐτοῦ·
    (his) children.'

Job argues, however, for punishment of the transgressor himself, saying (M 21:
19b-20a):

'Let him (God) recompense it unto him (the   ישלם אליו וידע
    wicked), that he (the wicked) may known it;
Let his own eyes see his destruction.'   יראו עינו כידו

Verse 19b continues God as subject of the verb ישלם, The suffix of אליו re-
--- ----------------------

[1]Cf., supra, p. 50f., for a full discussion of the method whereby G
obtains this reading.

fers to the wicked, and the subject of יֵדַע therefore is the wicked who is to know his own iniquity. Having taken God out of verse 19a, the translator feels that verse 19b has no place in the sequence of thought. He therefore omits the line, thereby removing the picture of a vengeful God. G accordingly proceeds from 19a to 20, rendering the first line:

'May his own eyes see his own slaughter.' ἴδοισαν οἱ ὀφθαλμοὶ αὐτοῦ τὴν ἑαυτοῦ σφαγήν.

Eliphaz now (chap. 21) inveighs against Job for the third time. He insists that Job has perpetrated wrongs against widows and orphans and that for this reason Job is now in such dire distress. Eliphaz presents the transcendence of God whose abode is above mankind. He accuses Job of believing that because of this distance between God and man the affairs of man are neither seen nor taken into account by God. He admonishes Job not to follow the path of the wicked (M 22:12-17a):

'Is not God as high as the heavens?	הֲלֹא־אֱלוֹהַ גֹּבַהּ שָׁמָיִם
And behold the topmost of the stars, how high they are!	וּרְאֵה רֹאשׁ כּוֹכָבִים כִּי־רָמּוּ
And thou sayest, What doth God know?	וְאָמַרְתָּ מַה־יָּדַע אֵל
Can he judge through the thick darkness?	הַבְעַד עֲרָפֶל יִשְׁפּוֹט
Thick clouds are a covering to him, that he seeth not;	עָבִים סֵתֶר־לוֹ וְלֹא יִרְאֶה
And he walketh on the vault of heaven.	וְחוּג שָׁמַיִם יִתְהַלָּךְ
Wilt thou keep the old way which wicked men did tread?	הַאֹרַח עוֹלָם תִּשְׁמוֹר אֲשֶׁר
Who were snatched away before their time,	דָּרְכוּ מְתֵי־אָוֶן
Whose foundation was poured out as a stream?	אֲשֶׁר־קֻמְּטוּ וְלֹא־עֵת
Who said unto God, Depart from us?'	נָהָר יוּצַק יְסוֹדָם
	הָאֹמְרִים לָאֵל סוּר מִמֶּנּוּ

The translator apparently wishes to avoid the comparison of God's loftiness to that of the heavens in line 1 of verse 12 because of its close association with God in line 1. G therefore rewrites the verse to emphasize the fact that God sees all things and humbles the insolent. By joining וּרְאֵה of line 2 to line 1, G obtains ἐφορᾷ 'he sees'. G renders אֱלוֹהַ גֹּבַהּ שָׁמַיִם by ὁ τὰ ὑψηλὰ ναίων 'he who dwelleth in the heights'. He rewrites line 2 to show that God does not allow the insolent to remain puffed-up, by playing with רם 'they are

high' which suggests רום 'height' and is translated as ὕβρις 'insolence'.

G then omits verses 13 and 14 because they suggest a limitation upon God.

Verses 13-16 also tend to detract from the character of Job. Verse 17a has

already been treated (p. 18). It should, however, be noted that in this line

οἱ λέγοντες 'those who say' refers back to τοὺς ὕβρει φερομένους 'those borne

along by insolence' of verse 12. G thus presents a natural sequence of thought

and reads:

'Does not he who dwelleth in the heights see?	μὴ οὐχὶ ὁ τὰ ὑψηλὰ ναίων ἐφορᾷ;
But he humbled those who are borne along by insolence,[1]	τοὺς δὲ ὕβρει φερομένους ἐταπείνωσεν,
Those who say, The Lord -- what will he do to us?'	οἱ λέγοντες Κύριος τί ποιήσει ἡμῖν;

In chapters 26 and 27 Job replies to the third speech of Bildad.

Job makes use of an ironical form of rebuttal against the argument of his three

companions. He employs the same phraseology as they had used. Job shows that,

if the wicked perish in the manner described by the three friends, then they

themselves also must take heed lest they be condemned for their malicious ac-

cusations of him. In the course of his description of the unhappy fate of trans-

gressors, , Job says concerning the wicked man (M 27:20-23):

'Terrors overtake him like waters;	תשיגהו כמים בלהות
In the night a whirlwind stealeth him away.	לילה גנבתו סופה
The sirocco carrieth him away, and he departeth;	ישאהו קדים וילך
And it sweepeth him out of his place.	וישערהו ממקמו
And he (God) hurleth at him and spareth not;	וישלך עליו ולא יחמל
He fleeth away from his (God's) hand.	מידו ברוח יברח
Men clap their hands at him,	ישפק עלימו כפימו
And hiss at him from his place.'	וישרק עליו ממקמו

----

[1]This interpretation does not accept the question mark at the end
of 12b in the texts of Rahlfs and Swete.

The translator renders בלהות of line 1 in verse 20 freely as αἱ ὀδύναι 'pains', thereby specifying what kind of terror reaches unto the wicked. In line 2 סופה is rendered as γνόφος 'darkness', -- a translation probably suggested by the fact that the sirocco is laden with dust -- which may imply death itself. Verse 21 of the Hebrew text adds no new thought to that of verse 20 and is accordingly omitted. G omits verse 22 which portrays God as pursuing man relentlessly. Verse 23 is awkward because of the change of subject from that of God to man. The object of contempt denoted by 'him' in verse 23 is probably the wicked man who is to be destroyed, but the meaning is not clear. G avoids any possibility of its referring to God by omitting the verse. The translator therefore concludes Job's speech and chapter 27 with verse 20:

'Pains encountered him like water,   συνήντησαν αὐτῷ ὥσπερ ὕδωρ αἱ ὀδύναι,
But in (the) night darkness stole him away.'νυκτὶ δὲ ὑφείλατο αὐτὸν γνόφος·

In Job's closing monologue (chaps. 29-31) he solemnly reasserts that there is no justification for God's violent treatment of him in the present as compared with the protection which God had vouchsafed him in the former days of prosperity. Job affirms that he has not sinned, even in his heart. He says (M 31:1-6):

'I made a covenant with mine eyes:	ברית כרתי לעיני
How then should I look upon a virgin?	ומה אתבונן על־בתולה
For what is the portion of God from above,	ומה חלק אלוה ממעל
And the heritage of the Almighty from on high?	ונחלת שדי ממרמים
Is it not calamity for the unrighteous,	הלא־איד לעול
And disaster for the workers of iniquity?	ונכר לפעלי און
Doth not he (God) see my ways	הלא־הוא יראה דרכי
And count all my steps?	וכל־צעדי יספור
If I have walked with insincerity,	אם־הלכתי עם־שוא
Or my foot hath hasted unto deceit,	ותחש על־מרמה רגלי
Let me be weighed in just scales,,	ישקלני במאזני־צדק
And let God know mine integrity.'	וידע אלוה תמתי

The Hebrew of verse 1 means that Job has not committed adultery even with his eyes, i. e., in his heart (cf., Matt. 5:27-29). Yet, even though verse 1 presents Job as a moral man, G objects to the idea that a covenant could be made

with a human eye.[1] Out of a high regard for the concept of the Sinai covenant,
therefore, G omits the verse. Verses 2 and 4 are omitted in order to keep God
out of the questionings of Job. Verse 3 in the Hebrew portrays God as wreak-
ing disaster. G feels that this detracts from the perfect character of God,
so it omits verse 3. G accordingly begins chapter 31 with verses 5 and 6:

'But if I had been walking with scorners, εἰ δὲ ἤμην πεπορευμένος μετὰ γελοι-
And if my foot hasted to deceit, αστῶν, εἰ δὲ καὶ ἐσπούδασεν ὁ πούς μου εἰς δόλον,
Then may he weigh me in a just scale; ἱσταίη με ἄρα ἐν ζυγῷ δικαίῳ,
But the Lord knows mine integrity.' οἶδεν δὲ ὁ κύριος τὴν ἀκακίαν μου.

In treating verse 6 of the Hebrew G makes God the agent of action in line 1.
The translator changes from the optative mood in the second to the indicative,
thereby making a statement of act which excludes any possibility that God would
need to be informed as to the integrity of Job.

  Elihu concludes his speech in chapters 36 and 37 by stressing the
necessity of a man's accepting suffering as a mark of God's discipline. Elihu
depicts God's instruction of man as follows (M 36:10-12):

'He openeth also their ear to instruction, ויגל אזנם למוסר
And commandeth that they return from iniquity. ויאמר כי־ישבון מאון
If they hearken and serve (him), אם־ישמעו ויעבדו
They shall spend their days in prosperity and יכלו ימיהם בטוב
 their years in pleasure. ושניהם בנעימים
But if they hearken not, they shall perish by ואם־לא ישמעו בשלח יעברו
 the sword,
And they shall die without knowledge.' ויגועו בבלי־דעת

The reason for G's rendering of verse 10 was discussed in Chapter II (pp. 37-38).
Apparently the translator objects to verses 11 and 12 because they imply that a
man may refuse God's warning which is addressed directly to them. He therefore avoids the possibility in line 1 of verse 12 of the Hebrew text that God
causes the wicked to perish by the sword. Instead he offers a reason why God

----

[1]Cf., Gehman, op. cit., p. 238, for a discussion of 5:23a where the
covenant with the stones of the field is avoided by the Greek translator.

will not save them: the ungodly do not want to know the Lord, even if they

have heard his instructions. G therefore omits verse 11 and changes verse 12,

reading:

'But he (God) will hearken to the just one . ἀλλὰ τοῦ δικαίου εἰσακούσεται·
But the ungodly ones he will not save alive, ἀσεβεῖς δὲ οὐ διασῴζει παρὰ τὸ μὴ
  because they do not want to know the Lord, βούλεσθαι εἰδέναι αὐτοὺς τὸν κύριον
And because, being admonished, they were not καὶ διότι νουθετούμενοι ἀνήκοοι
  willing to heard.' ἦσαν.

G thus presents the wicked as unrepentant transgressors.

      When God answers Job (chaps. 38-40) out of the tempest, he cites the

examples of his majestic power in ordaining the works of the universe. God shows

the finitude of Job by asking him whether he has recognized who it is who has

caused the rain to fall upon even barren ground (M 38:25-28):

'Who hath cleft a channel for the raincloud, מי־פלג לשטף תעלה
Or a way for the lighthing of the thunder? ודרך לחזיז קלות
To cause it to rain upon a land where no man is, להמטיר על־ארץ לא־איש
Or the wilderness, wherein there is no man? מדבר לא־אדם בו
To satisfy devastation and desolation, להשביע שאה ומשאה
And to cause to sprout the growing-place of young ולהצמיח מצא דשא
  grass?
Hath the rain a father, היש־למטר אב
Or who hath begotten the drops of dew?' או מי־הוליד אגלי־טל

The translator gives a good rendering of verse 25, representing תעלה by ῥύσις

'stream'; לשטף by ὑετῷ λάβρῳ 'for turbulent water'; and לחזיז קלות by κυδοιμοί

'uproarings, turbulences'. G omits verses 26 and 27 to avoid any suggestion

that God would perform such an apparently foolish thing as causing it to rain

upon a desolate and abandoned land. The sequence of verses 25 and 28 is thus

a perfectly natural one in G:

'But who hath prepared a stream for tur- τίς δὲ ἡτοίμασεν ὑετῷ λάβρῳ ῥύσιν,
  bulent water,
And a way for uproarings (lightning and ὁδὸν δὲ κυδοιμῶν
  thunder)?
Who is the father of rain? τίς ἐστιν ὑετοῦ πατήρ;
But who is the one who hath begotten the τίς δὲ ἐστιν ὁ τετοκὼς βώλους δρόσου;
  drops of dew?'

      Yahweh then discusses his omniscience in the realm of animal life.

He asks Job (M 38:41-39:1):

'Who provideth for the raven-his prey,   מי יכין לערב צידו
When his young ones cry unto God   כי־ילדו אל־אל ישועו
And wander for lack of food?[1]   יתעו לבלי־אבל
Knowest thou the time of the bringing forth of הידעת עת לדת יעלי־סלע
    the rock-goats?
Or canst thou mark when the hinds do calve?'   חלל אילות תשמר

In the third line of 38:41 the translator freely renders לבלי־אבל with τὰ σῖτα
ζητοῦντεζ. Certainly this is the meaning of the Hebrew, but G is more matter-
of-fact in stating the reason for the wandering about of the young birds. Apparently the translator objects to God's asking Job in 39:1a whether he knows
the 'time of the bringing forth' of the goats, since the translator interprets
עת לדת in the sense of heat (*Liebeslust*). He therefore omits the line as in-
delicate. In line 2 חלל is rendered freely as ὠδῖνας 'pains', with the meaning
of the line the same as that of the Hebrew. G thus presents a good transition
from 38:41 to 39:1b and reads:

'But who hath prepared food for the raven?   τίς δὲ ἡτοίμασεν κόρακι βοράν;
For its young ones have cried out to the Lord,νεοσσοὶ γὰρ αὐτοῦ πρὸς κύριον κεκρά-
Wandering about, seeking food.   γασιν, πλανώμενοι τὰ σῖτα ζητοῦντες.
But hast thou observed the pains of the hind?'ἐφύλαξαζ δὲ ὠδῖνας ἐλάφων;

      Not only does the translator omit passages that cast reflections upon
the perfect character of God, but he also leaves out verses which are not in line
with his concept of death or with his understanding of the character of the man
Job:

The Concept of Death and the Character of Job

      When Job delivers his closing monologue (chaps. 29-31), he recounts

---

[1]Budde, op. cit., ad loc., emends יתעו to יתעה 'he wanders about' because '. . . יעו' passt schlecht zu den jungen Raben, da von einem 'Traumeln'
vor Hunger nicht der Rede sein kann. Der alte Vogel fliegt ratlos umher, um,
den Jungen Atzung zu schaffen.' Duhm, op. cit., ad loc., also emends to יעו'
for the following reason: 'יעו' lässt sich nicht als Prädikat zu ילדו' verstehen,
denn die Jungen, die noch von den Alten gefüttert werden, irren nicht umher, son-
dern bleiben in die Höhle.' The writer, however, retains the reading יעו' as
translated above. G also reads יעו', not יעו',

his former days of prosperity when he had looked forward to spending his de-

clining years in honour and prosperity. Job recalls his thoughts in those past

days (M 29:18-21):

'Then I said, I shall die with my nest,	ואמר עם־קני אגוע
And I shall myltiply my days as sand,	בחול ארבה ימים
My root open unto the waters;	שרשי פתוח אלי־מים
And dew will stay all night upon my branch,	וטל ילין בקצירי
My glory fresh within me;	כבודי חדש עמדי
And my bow shall show newness (shall be renewed) in my hand.	וקשתי בידי תחליף
Unto me men gave ear and waited	לי־שמעו ויחלו
And kept silence for my counsel.'	וידמו למו עצתי

The translator freely renders line 1 of verse 18 to express the same idea of

long life as that of the Hebrew. The interpretation of line 2, however, is

more complex. G apparently wishes to avoid the mythology attached to reading

חול 'sand' as חול 'phoenix.'.The translator, however, wishes to express the

idea of long life, so he uses στέλεχος φοίνικος 'trunk of the palm tree' for

חול to give this idea. In late Hebrew חול has two meanings: (1) sand; and

(2) the phoenix bird.[1] The more usual word for phoenix in late Hebrew is

אורשנא or אושינא. בחול in M therefore means 'as sand' in the sense of 'for a

long time'.[2] It is, nevertheless, the opinion of this writer that the reading

φοίνιξ came about in the first place because in Jewish literature חול came to

identified with the   phoenix. That G intended the word φοίνιξ to mean 'palm',

not 'phoenix', is seen by the fact that it added the word στέλεχος 'trunk' to

----

[1]Cf., Jacob Levy, *Neuhebräisches und Chaldäisches Wörterbuch über die Talmudim und Midraschim* (Leipzig: F. A. Brockhaus, 1876), and Marcus Jastrow, *A Dictionary of the Targumim, the Talmud Babli and Yerushalmi, and the Midrashic Literature* (London: Luzac & Co., 1903), s.v.

[2]The Targum reads for this line: והיך חלא אסני יומיא 'and like the sand I shall multiply my days', Ehrlich, *op. cit.*, ad loc., reads '. . . (ich) würde so viele Jahren leben, wie der Sandkörner sind'. Concerning this verse Dhorme, *op. cit.*, p. 390, comments: 'On connaît de reste les traditions des classiques sur le phénix. Quelques modernes se sont rangés à l'interprétation de l'école juive et ont traduit חול par 'comme le phénix' (Hitzig, Ewald, Budde, Duhm). Mais Bochart avait déjà prouvé que la légende rabbinique repose sur l'interprétation de חול par 'palmier'. Dhorme is correct in stating that both Duhm and Budde translate כחול as 'like the phoenix'.

make certain that φοίνιξ would not be interpreted as phoenix (the bird). In
other words, both the Hebrew and the Greek texts depict Job as having the hope
of long life. G then omits the figures of speech in verses 19 and 20 and resumes the description of Job's former prosperity by a free translation of verse
21. G reads:

'Then I said, My age will grow old;   εἶπα δέ 'Η ἡλικία μου γηράqει,
As the trunk of the palm I shall live ὥσπερ στέλεχος φοίνικος πολὺν χρόνον βιώσω·
    much time.
Hearing me, they paid attention,   ἐμοῦ ἀκούσαντες προσέσχον,
But they kept silence at my counsel.' ἐσιώπησαν δὲ ἐπὶ τῇ ἐμῇ βουλῇ·

In other words G avoids the concept of immortality such as that which the
legendary figure of the phoenix represents. Instead G makes certain that verse
18 denotes only a long life for Job.

In chapter 20 Sophar, lacking sympathy for the afflictions of Job,
denounces the wicked and asserts their ultimate doom. Job replies (chap. 21)
that quite the opposite is true. He cites the fact that transgressors usually
escape their just condemnation on earth. But Job does not lose faith in his
confidence in God as judge. With his three comrades in mind Job asks (M 21:
22-25) :

'Will any teach God knowledge? הלאל ילמד־דעת
Seeing it is he (God) who judgeth those that והוא רמים ישפוט
    are high?
One dieth in his very completeness, זה ימות בעצם תמו
Being wholly at ease and quiet. כלו שלאנן ושליו
His pails are full of milk, עטיניו מלאו חלב
And the marrow of his bones is moistened. ומח עצמתיו ישקה
And another dieth with a bitter soul, וזה ימות בנפש מרה
And hath never tasted of good.' ולא־אכל בטובה

The treatment of verse 22a was considered in Chapter I (p. 8). In 22b כמים suggests the plural of late Hebrew כמ 'deceiver', which is translated as φόνους
'murders'. G omits verse 23, probably because in 1:8 and 2:3 the adjective תם
is applied to Job as a clear indication of his uprightness before God. G
thus avoids any possible application of verse 23 to Job. G renders verse 24

freely which in context with verse 25 shows that even though the wicked may pros-

per, his end is pain and bitterness. G thus portrays Job as less cynical than

does the Hebrew text. G reads:

'Is not the Lord he who teaches insight and understanding?	πότερου οὐχὶ ὁ κυριός ἐστιν ὁ διδάσκων σύνεσιν καὶ ἐπιστήμην;
But he will decide murders.	αὐτὸς δὲ φόνους διακρινεῖ.
But his (the murderer's) entrails are full of fat;	τὰ δὲ ἔγκατα αὐτοῦ ἀλήρη·στέατος,
And his marrow is dissolved.	μυελὸς δὲ αὐτοῦ διαχεῖται.
But he dies in bitterness of soul,	ὁ δὲ τελευτᾷ ὑπὸ πικρίας ψυχῆς
Not eating any good.'	οὐ φαγὼν οὐδὲν ἀγαθόν.

In two instances the translator omits passages which confuses the

meaning of the text. As the concluding theme of this chapter, these examples

will be considered under the title which follows:

Clarification

In the wisdom poem of chapter 28 the work of miners is described in

some detail. Concerning the miners themselves there is the following reference

made (M 28:4-10):[1]

'He (the miner) breaketh open a shaft away from where men sojourn;	פרץ נחל מעם־גר
They (the miners) are forgotten of the foot (that passeth by);	הנתכחים מני־רגל
They hang afar from men; they swing to and fro.	דלו מאנוש נעו
As for the earth, out of it cometh bread;	ארץ ממנה יצא־לחם
And underneath, it is turned up as it were by fire.	ותחתיה נהפה כמו־אש
Its stones are the place of sapphires,	מקום־ספיר אבניה
And it hath dust of gold.	ועפרת זהב לו
That path, no bird of prey knoweth;	נתיב לא־ידעו עיט
Neither hath the falcon's eye seen it;	לא שזפתו עין איה
The proud beasts have not trodden it,	לא־הדריכהו בני־שחץ
Nor hath the lion passed thereby.	לא־עדה עליו שחל
He (the miner) putteth forth his hand upon the flinty rock;	בחלמיש שלח ידו
He (the miner) overturneth mountains by the roots;	הפך משרש הרים

----

[1]Cf., Leroy Waterman, 'Note on Job 28:4', *Journal of Biblical Litera-ture*, LXXI (September, 1952), 167-170, for an argument supporting the use of artificial lighting in mines during the post-exilic period and a different interpretation of the Hebrew.

He cutteth out channels among the rocks;	בצורות יארים בקע
And every precious thing his eye seeth.'	וכל־יקר ראתה עינו

G ascribes the action of verses 3 and 4 to God. In 9b G also glorifies God by
ascribing the action to him. Verses 5-9a with their description of the mine itself, therefore, break the sequence of thought as determined by G and are accordingly omitted. G translates 10a freely, and 10b has already been discussed
in connection with anti-anthropomorphisms (pp. 33-34). G accordingly renders:

'But those who forget the right path, became weak among mortals.	οἱ δὲ ἐπιλανθανόμενοι ὁδὸν δικαίαν ἠσθένησαν ἐκ βροτῶν.
But he (God) overturned mountains by the roots;	κατέστρεψεν δὲ ἐκ ῥιζῶν ὄρη·
Moreover, he let loose whirlpools of rivers,	δίνας δὲ ποταμῶν ἔρρηξεν,
And every prized thing mine (the poet's) eye hath seen.'	πᾶν δὲ ἔντιμον εἶδέν μου ὁ ὀφθαλμός·

In Elihu's lengthy discourse (chaps. 32-37), the words of advice
which Bildad, Ṣophar, and Eliphaz had given to Job are repeated. Elihu exhorts
the wise to make use of their intellectual power of discrimination to choose
what is right as opposed to Job's irreligious assertions. Elihu says (M 34:
2-5):

'Hear my words, ye wise men;	שמעו חכמים מלי
And give ear unto me, ye that have know-ledge.	וידעים האזינו לי
For the ear trieth words,	כי־אזן מלין תבחן
As the palate tasteth food.	וחך יטעם לאכל
Let us choose for ourselves that which is right;	משפט נבחרה־לנו
Let us know among ourselves what is good.	נדעה בינינו מה־טוב
For Job hath said: 'I am righteous,	כי־אמר איוב צדקתי
And God hath taken away my right;'	ואל הסיר משפטי

Verses 3 and 4 seem to obstruct the flow of thought. G may consider these
verses as too verbose or as rather irrelevant and omits them, thereby presenting a more matter-of-fact sequence. A more important reason for the omission,
however, is that G objects to the presumptuous idea in verse 4 that a man
may himself choose משפט in the sense of 'true religion'. G accordingly renders:

'Hear me, ye wise;	'Ακούσατέ μου, σοφοί·
Ye understanding ones, hearken unto that which is beautiful;	ἐπιστάμενοι, ἐνωτίζεσθε τὸ καλόν·
For Job hath said, I am righteous;	ὅτι εἴρηκεν Ἰώβ, Δίκαιός εἰμι,
The Lord hath deprived me of (my) judgment.	ὁ κύριος ἀπήλλαξέν μου τὸ κρίμα.

In this way the translator avoids any extraneous material and goes directly to
the heart of the matter.

The examples discussed in this chapter illustrate the fact that the
translator omits certain passages which are not in accord with his theological
method of exegesis. Whenever G omits a passage, whether it be to tone down,
avoid anthropomorphisms, eliminate expressions suggesting a reflection upon
God's character, delineate its concept of death, enhance Job's character, or
clarify a passage, the sequence of thought in the lines which are retained remains logical. In other words G makes a smooth transition from the verse immediately preceding to the verse immediately following any omitted passage.
An examination of the reasons why the translator omits certain passages yields
further evidence for an understanding of the theological method followed by
the translator in his treatment of the Hebrew text of Job. Such a study proves
that G is not based upon a *Vorlage* far different from that of M, but that the
text of M is very close to the one used by the Greek translator in his work
on the Book of Job.

CHAPTER V

CONCLUSION

The writer has presented in the preceding chapters the results of
his study of the Old Greek text of Job in comparison with the Hebrew. In pre-
paration for this work the Vulgate and Targum of Job, together with rabbinic
exegesis, were also examined, but nothing was found which affects the conclusions of the writer's thesis.

The two assumptions which governed this study are that (a) the
translator who rendered the Book of Job into Greek had a good knowledge of Hebrew, and (b) the translator tried to make sense out of the passages which were
before him. For these reasons every case in which G differs from M was carefully examined to see why there was a departure from the Hebrew text. In some
instances there was found a change which could be attributed to an error of
the eye: the reading of ד for ר, י for ו, ו for ן, or ב for כ. Some of
these changes may have been made deliberately through a trick of the translator. In other cases there were found differences which could be explained as
caused by an unpointed Hebrew text written continuously without word and verse
divisions. In every such instance the collations of MSS by Kennicott and De
Rossi were consulted together with the variant readings of Holmes and Parsons
in order to discover what the translator of the Hebrew had read and translated.
As a result it was seen that for the Book of Job the translator had a Hebrew
text not far different from that of the Masoretes. This means that there are
a large number of deviations from the Hebrew which cannot be explained as due

91

to double readings in the Hebrew tradition or on the basis of textual grounds
alone. The conclusion is that such differences are deliberate. The reasons
for the changes constituted the body of this monograph.

The translator is seen to follow an exegetical method of approach
to the Hebrew text. He interprets passages or expressions according to a pattern which has a theological foundation. The word 'pattern' does not denote
a rigid system of rules such as those which govern historical exegesis. It
means rather an ideal concerning God and man's relation to him which colours
the exegesis of the translator. As a result there are many cases in G which
show both extreme literalism and great freedom of rendering by the translator
in the same verse or adjacent verses. This apparent anomaly is best understood
by considering the translator's theology which has left its mark on G. Thus
it is that in G there avoided ideas which are theologically offensive to the
translator, such as concepts of God in the Hebrew text which seem to suggest
that man may be arrogant before God (Chapter I). Although it cannot be assumed that the translator set out to remove all anthropomorphisms, there are
numerous examples which show that anti-anthropomorphisms enter into his theological pattern of exegesis (Chapter II). Another tendency seen in G is that
of avoiding reflection upon the perfect character of God. Thus it is that
the translator tends to lessen the force of destructive action which is as-
cribed to God in the Hebrew text (Chapter III). If the translator cannot pur-
sue these tendencies by a departure from a literal rendering of the Hebrew
text, he does so by omitting passages or expressions which are contrary to
his theological interpretation. He attempts, however, to make a good sequence
so that incases of an omission from the Hebrew, G presents a logical order
of thought (Chapter IV).

The examples presented in Chapters I-IV fall for the most part quite naturally into the general categories under which they are listed. The examination of the evidence shows that the translator, a representative of the Hellenistic-Jewish circles, in working on the Hebrew text of Job used a *Vorlage* which was close to that of M. Thus it was seen that the logical reason for the changes which the translator made in rendering this *Vorlage* into Greek is that he followed a method of exegesis which is governed by a theological approach.

The value of these conclusions for LXX studies in general are many. The footnotes in the *Biblia Hebraica*[1] often advise the student to 'read with the Greek','or 'delete with the Greek', but, for the Book of Job such procedure is misleading. Up to the time of Gehman's article in the *Journal of Biblical Literature*[2] most LXX studies had been governed by the idea that a departure from a literal rendering of the Hebrew was due for the most part to the literary style of the translator or to a different *Vorlage*. It is hoped that the publication of this work will add further proof for holding that the *Vorlage* behind the LXX of Job differs but little from that of M, and that haphazard literary style alone cannot account for the differences between G and M. Finally, this investigation of the Book of Job, if supplemented by a similar work on other books of the Old Testament, should be a contribution toward a clearer understanding of the exegetical method used by the LXX translators.

--------- ---

[1]Kittel, *op. cit.*

[2]*Op. cit.*

APPENDIX

Registry of Verses

APPENDIX

BIBLIOGRAPHY

Texts

De Rossi, Johannis B. (ed.). *Psalmi, Proverbia, Iob, Daniel, Ezras, Nehemia, Chronica, Seu Paralip., Appendix.* Vol. IV of *Variae Lectiones Veteris Testamenti ex Immensa MSS.* 4 vols. Parmae: Ex Regio Typographio, 1784.

Grabe, Joannes Ernestus (ed.). *Septuaginta Interpretum Tomus I-IV.* Vol. III, *IOB.* Oxonii: E Theatro Sheldiano, 1707-1709.

Hetzenaver, P. Michael (ed.). *Biblia Sacra - Vulgatae Editionis.* Oenipotente: Sumptibus Librariae Accademicae Wagnerianae, 1906.

Holmes, Robertus, and Parsons, Jacobus. *Vetus Testamentum Graecum cum variis lectionibus.* Vol. III. Oxonii: A Typographio Clarendoniano, 1823.

Kennicott, Benjaminus (ed.). *Vetus Testamentum Graecum cum Variis Lectionibus.* 2 vols. Oxonii: E Typographeo Clarendoniano, 1776.

Kittel, Rudolf (ed.). *Biblia Hebraica.* 3d ed. Stuttgart: Wurttembergische Bibelanstalt, 1937.

Rahlfs, Alfred (ed.). *Libri poetici et prophetici.* Vol. II of *Septuaginta id est Vetus Testamentum Graece Iuxta LXX Interpretes.* 2 vols. Stuttgart: Wurttembergische Bibelanstalt, 1935.

Soisalon-Soininen. I. *Die Textformen der Septuaginta-Übersetzung des Richterbuches.* Helsinki: Druckerer - A. G. der Finnischen Literaturgesellschaft, 1951.

Swete, Henry Barclay (ed.). *The Old Testament in Greek According to the Septuagint.* 3 vols. Cambridge: University Press, 1891.

Walton, Brian (ed.). *Biblia Sacra Polyglota Complectentia.* 6 vols. London: Thomas Roycroft, 1656-1657.

Lexicons and Concordances

Brown, F., Driver, S. R., and Briggs, C. A. *A Hebrew and English Lexicon of the Old Testament.* Boston: Houghton, Mifflin & Co., 1906.

Gesenius, Wilhelm. *Hebräisches und Aramäisches Handwörterbuch uber das Alte Testament.* 17th ed. revised by Frants Buhl. Berlin: Springer Verlag, 1949.

Hatch, Edwin, and Redpath, Henry. *A Concordance to the Septuagint and the other*

Greek Versions of the Old Testament (Including the Apocryphal Books).
3 vols. Oxford: Clarendon Press, 1897.

Jastrow, Marcus. *A Dictionary of the Targumin, the Talmud Babli and Yerushalmi,
and the Midrashic Literature.* 2 vols. London: Luzac & Co., 1903.

Koehler, Ludwig, and Baumgartner, Walter. *Lexicon in Veteris Testamenti Libros.*
Through הכפה. Parts I-XII. Leiden: E. J. Brill, 1948-1952.

Krauss, Samuel. *Griechische und lateinische Lehnwörter im Talmud, Midrasch und
Targum.* Berlin, 1898.

Levy, Jacob. *Neuhebräisches und Chaldäisches Wörterbuch über die Talmudim und
Midraschim.* 3 vols. Leipzig: F. A. Brockhaus, 1876.

Schleusner, Ioh. F. *Novus Thesaurus philogico-criticus sive Lexicon in LXX et
Reliquous Interpretes graecos ac scriptores apocryphos Veteris Testamenti.* 5 vols. Leipsig: In Libraria Weidmannia, 1820-1821.

Commentaries

Arnheim, H. *Das Buch Hiob übersetzt und vollständig commentiert.* Glogau: H.
Prausnitz, 1836.

Ball, C J. *The Book of Job: A Revised Text and Version.* Oxford: Clarendon
Press, 1922.

Beer, Georg. *Der Text des Buches Hiob.* Marburg: N. G. Elwertsche Buchhandlung, 1897.

Bickell, Gustav. *Das Buch Iob nach Anleitung der Strophik und der Septuaginta.*
Wien: Carl Gerold's Sohn, 1894.

Budde, Karl. *Das Buch Hiob.* Part II, Vol. I of *Handkommentar zum Alten Testament.* Edited by D. W. Nowack. Gottingen: Vandenhoeck & Ruprecht, 1896.

Buttenwieser, Moses. *The Book of Job.* New York: The Macmillan Co., 1922.

Davidson, A. B. *The Book of Job.* In *The Cambridge Bible for Schools and Col-
leges.* Old Testament edited by A. F. Kirkpatrick. Cambridge: University
Press, 1937.

Delitzsch, Franz. *Das Buch Iob.* Vol. II of *Biblischer Commentar über die
Poetischen Bücher des Alten Testament.* In *Biblischer Commentar über
das Alte Testament.* Edited by C. F. Keil and Franz Delitzsch. Leipzig:
Dorffling & Franke, 1876.

Dhorme, Paul. *Le Livre de Job.* Published by J. Gabalda. Paris: Librarie Victor
Lecoffre, 1926.

Dillmann, August. *Hiob.* In *Kurzgefasstes exegetisches Handbuch zum Alten Testament.* 4th ed. Leipzig: S. Hirzel, 1891.

Driver, S. R., and Gray, G. B. *A Critical and Exegetical Commentary on the Book of Job together with a new Translation*. In *The International Critical Commentary on the Old and New Testaments*. 2 vols. New York: Charles Scribner's Sons, 1921.

Duhm, Bernhard. *Das Buch Hiob*. Vol. XVI of *Kurzer Hand-Commentar zum Alten Testament*. Edited by Karl Marti. 20 vols. Freiburg I. B.: J. C. B. Mohr (Paul Siebeck), 1897-1904.

Eerdmans, B. D. *Studies in Job*. 2 vols. Leiden: Burgersdijk & Niermans Templum Salomonis, 1939.

Ehrlich, Arnold B. *Psalmen, Sprüche und Hiob*. Vol. VI of *Randglossen zur Hebräischen Bibel*. Leipzig: J. C. Hinrichs'sche Buchhandlung, 1913.

Ewald, Heinrich. *Das Buch Ijob*. Part III of *Die Dichter des Alten Testaments*. Gottingen: Vandenhoeck & Ruprecht, 1854.

Grill, Julius. *Zur Kritik der Komposition des Buches Hiob*. Tubingen: L. F. Fues'sche Buchdruckerei, 1890.

Hengstenberg, Ernst Wilhelm. *Das Buch Hiob erläutert*. 2 vols. Leipzig: J. C. Hinrichs'sche Buchhandlung , 1875.

Hitzig, Ferdinand. *Das Buch Hiob übersetzt und ausgelegt*. Leipzig: C. F. Winter'sche Verlagshandlung, 1874.

Holscher, Gustav. *Das Buch Hiob*. Series 1, Vol. XVII of *Handbuch zum Alten Testament*. Tubingen: J. C. B. Mohr (Paul Siebeck), 2nd ed., 1952.

Hoffmann, Johann Georg Ernst. *Hiob nach Johann Georg Ernst Hoffmann*. Kiel: C. F. Haeseler, 1891.

Hufnagel, Wilhelm Friedrich. *Hiob - neu übersetzt mit Anmerkungen*. Erlangen: Palmische Buchhandlung, 1781.

Junker, H. *Job*. Vol. XIII (together with *Sirach* by V. Hamp) of *Die Heilige Schrift in deutschen Übersetzung, Echter-Bibel: Das Alte Testament*. Edited by F. Nötscher. Würzburg: Echter Verlag, 1951.

Kissane, Edward J. *The Book of Job Translated From a Critically Revised Hebrew Text With a Commentary*. Dublin: Brown & Nol an Ltd., 1939.

Knabenbauer, Iosephus. *Commentarius in Librum Iob*. Part II, Vol. I of *Cursus Scripturae Sacrae*. Edited by R. Cornely, I. Knabenbauer, and Fr, de Hummdauer. Paris: P. Lethielleux, 1886.

König, Eduard. *Das Buch Hiob eingeleitet, übersetzt und erklärt*. Gütersloh: C. Bertelsmann ,1929.

Lassen, Abraham L. *The Commentary of Levi ben Gerson (Gersonides) on the Book of Job*. New York: Bloch Publishing Co., 1946.

Lindblom, Joh. *Bokem om Job och hans lidande.* Lund: C. W. K. Gleerups Forlag, 1940.

Merx, Adalbert. *Das Gedicht von Hiob: Hebräischer Text, Kritisch Bearbeitet und Uebersetzt, Nebst Sachlicher Und Kritischer Einleitung.* Jena: Mauke's Verlag (Hermann Dufft), 1871.

Reichert, Victor E. *Job with Hebrew Text and English Translation.* In the *Soncino Books of the Bible.* Edited by A. Cohen. Hindhead, Surrey: Soncino Press, 1946.

Schlottmann, Konstantin. *Das Buch Hiob verdeutscht und erläutert.* Berlin: Wiegandt & Brieben, 1851.

Schultens, Albert. *Liber Jobi cum Nova Versione ad Hebraeum fontem et Commentario Perpetuo.* Lugundi Batavorum: Johannem Luzac, 1737.

Strahan, James. *The Book of Job Interpreted.* Edinburgh: T. & T. Clark, 1913.

Strickel, Johann Gustav. *Das Buch Hiob.* Leipzig: Weidmann'sche Buchhandlung, 1842.

Studer, Gottlieb Ludwig. *Das Buch Hiob.* Bremen: Verlag von M. Heinsius, 1881.

Umbreit, F. W. C. *Das Buch Hiob: Uebersetzung und Auslegung.* Heidelberg: J. C. B. Mohr, 1824.

Von Winterfield. *Commentar über Das Buch Iob.* Leipzig: Verlag von Hermann Walter, 1898.

Vuilleumer, H. *Le livre de Job.* Lausanne: F. Rouge, 1894.

Weiser, Artur. *Das Buch Hiob.* Part XIII of *Das Alte Testament Deutsch.* Gottingen: Vandenhoeck & Ruprecht, 1951.

Wright, G. H. Bateson. *The Book of Job.* London: Williams & Norgate, 1883.

General Works

Ancessi, Victor. *Job et l'Égypte Le Rédempteur et la Vie Future.* Paris: Ernest Leroux, 1877.

Bentzen, Aage. *Introduction to the Old Testament.* 2 vols. Copenhagen: G. E. C. Gads Forlag, 1948.

Bickell, Gustav. *Carmina Veteris Testamenti Metrice: Notas Criticas et Dissertationem De Re Metrica Hebraeorum.* Oneniponte: In Libraria Academica Wagneriana, 1882.

Bochart, Samuel. *Hierozoicon, sive de animalibus . . scripturae.* 3 vols. Edited by E. F. C. Rosenmuller. Leipzig: In Libraria Weidmann, 1793.

Cheyne, Thomas Kelly. *Job and Solomon or The Wisdom of the Old Testament.* London: Kegan Paul, Trench & Co., 1887.

De Wette, Wilhelm M. L. *Die Einleitung in das Alte Testament.* Part I of *Lehrbuch der historisch-kritischen Einleitung in die Bibel Alten und Neuen Testaments.* 6th ed. Berlin: G. Reimer, 1845.

Driver, S. R. *An Introduction to the Literature of the Old Testament.* New York: Charles Scribner's Sons, 1942.

------------. *The Book of Job in the Revised Version.* Oxford: Clarendon Press, 1906.

Eichhorn, Johann Gottfried.. *Einleitung in das Alte Testament.* 3 vols. 3d ed. Leipzig: Weidmannischen Buchhandlung, 1803.

Frankel, Z. *Vorstudien zu der Septuaginta.* Vol. I, Part I of *Historisch-Kritische Studien zu der Septuaginta nebst Beiträgen zu den Targumim.* Leipzig: F. C. W. Vogel, 1841.

Frieländer, M. *Griechische Philosophie im Alten Testament: Eine Einleitung in Die Psalmen- Und Weisheitsliteratur.* Berlin: Georg Reimer, 1904.

Gailey, James Herbert, Jr. *Jerome's Latin Version of Job from the Greek (Chaps. 1-26): Its Text, Character, and Provenance.* Princeton: Princeton Theological Seminary Pamphlet Series, 1945.

Gerleman, Gillis. *Studies in the Septuagint.* Vol. I, *Book of Job.* ('Lunds Universitets Årsskrift,' N. F., Avd. 1, Bd. 43, No. 2). Lund : C. W. K. Gleerup, 1946.

Giesebrecht, Friedrich. *Der Wendepunkt des Buches Hiob: Capitel 27 und 28.* Berlin: Eugen Grosser, 1879.

Ginsburg, Christian D. *Introduction to the Massoretico-Critical Edition of the Hebrew Bible.* London: Trinitarian Bible Society, 1897.

Graetz, H. *Emendationes in plerosque sacrae Scripturae Veteris Teetamenti Libros.* 3 vols. Breslau, 1892.

Houbigant, Carl F. *Notae criticae in universos Veteris Testamenti Libros cum hebraice, tum graece scriptos, cum integris euisdem prolegomenis.* 2 vols. Francofurti ad Moenum: Varrentrapp Filium & Wenner, 1777.

Jastrow, Morris, Jr. *The Book of Job: its Origin, Growth, and Interpretation.* Philadelphia: J. B. Lippincott Co., 1920.

Kautzsch, Karl. *Das sogenannte Volksbuch von Hiob und der Ursprung von Hiob Cap. I, II, XLII, 7-17.* Tübingen: Verlage von J. C. B. Mohr (Paul Siebeck), 1900.

Kraeling, Emil G. *The Book of the Ways of God.* New York: Charles Scribner's Sons, 1938.

Lagarde, Paul de. *Gesammelte Abhandlungen.* Leipzig: F. A. Brockhaus, 1866.

Le Hir, M. L'Abbé. *Le Livre de Job.* Paris: Jouby et Roger, 1873.

Lindblom, Joh. *La Composition du Livre de Job.* Lund: C. W. K. Gleerups Förlag, 1945.

Loisy, A. *Le Livre de Job Traduit De L'Hébreu Avec Une Introduction.* Amiens: Imprimerie Rousseau-Leroy, 1892.

Pfeiffer, Robert H. *Introduction to the Old Testament.* 3d ed. New York: Harper & Bros., 1941.

Prijs, Leo. *Jüdische Tradition in der Septuaginta.* Leiden: E. J. Brill, 1948.

Renan, Ernest. *Le Livre De Job Traduit De L'Hébreu Avec Une Etude Sur L'Age Et Le Caractere Du Poeme.* 5th ed. Edited by Calmann Levy. Paris: A La Librarie Nouvelle. 1894.

Reuss, Eduard. *Religions-und Moralphilosophie der Hebräer.* Vol. VI of *Das Alte Testament übersetzt, eingeleitet und erläutert.* Braunschweig: D. A. Schwetschke & Sohn, 1894.

Richter, Georg. *Erläuterungen zu dunkeln Stellen im Buche Hiob.* Vol. XI of *Beiträge zur Wissenschaft vom Alten Testament.* Edited by Rudolf Kittel. Leipzig: J. C. Hinrichs'sche Buchhandlung, 1912.

Rosenmuller, Ernst. *Scholia in Job.* Vols. I-II, Part V of *Scholia in Vetus Testamentum.* 2d ed. revised. Leipzig: Sumptibus Ios. Ambros. Barthii, 1795.

Schnurrer, Christian Friedrich. *Animadversiones ad quaedam loca Iobi.* Tubingen: Literis Sigmundianis, 1781.

Sellin, Ernst. *Das Problem des Hiobbuches.* Leipzig: A. Deichert'sche Verlagsbuchhandlung, Werner School, 1919.

Stevenson, Wm. Barron. *The Poem of Job: A Literary Study with a New Translation.* London: British Academy, 1947.

Stuhlmann, Matthias Henrich. *Hiob: Ein religiöses Gedicht.* Hamburg: Friedrich Perthes, 1804.

Vischer, Wilhelm. *Hiob: Ein Zeuge Jesu Christi.* 5th ed. Zürich: Evangelischer Verlag, 1942.

Volz, Paul. *Weisheit (Das Buch Hiob, Sprüche und Jesus Sirach, Prediger).* Vol. II, Part III of *Die Schriften des Alten Testaments in Auswahl neu übersetzt und für die Gegenwart erklärt.* Edited by H. Gressmann, H. Gunkel, M. Haller, H. Schmidt, W. Stark, and Paul Volz. Gottingen: Vandenhoeck & Ruprecht, 1911.

Wemyss ,Thomas. *Job and His Times: or a Picture of the Patriarchal Age.* London: Jackson & Walford, 1839.

Articles

Alfrink, Bernhard. 'Die Bedeutung des Wortes גוע in Job 21,33 und 38,38,' *Biblica*, XIII (1932), 77-86.

Barmstark, A. 'Neue orientalische Probleme biblischer Textgeschichte,' *Zeitschrift der Deutschen Morgenländischen Gesellschaft*, LXXXIX (1935), 89-118.

Barton, George A. 'Some text-critical notes on Job,' *Journal of Biblical Literature*, XLII (1923), 29-32.

Beer, Georg. 'Textkritische Studien zum Buche Job,' *Zeitschrift für die Alttestamentliche Wissenschaft*, XVI (1896), 297-314; XVII (1897), 97-122; XVIII (1898), 257-86.

Bertram, Georg. 'Der Begriff Religion in der Septuaginta,' *Zeitschrift der Deutschen Morgenländischen Gesellschaft*, NF XII (1934), 1-5.

----------. 'Theologische Prägungen von ἁμαρτία in LXX,' *Theologisches Wörterbuch zum Neuen Testament*. Edited by Gerhard Kittel. Vol. I, 1932.

Bickell, G. 'Der ursprüngliche Septuagintatext des Buches Job,",' *Zeitschrift für Katholische Theologie*, X (1886), 557-64.

Boehmer, J. 'Mitteilung: Was ist der Sinn von Hiob 39:13-18 an seiner gegenwärtigen Stelle?,' *Zeitschrift für die Alttestamentliche Wissenschaft*, LIII (1935), 289- 91.

Bruston, C. 'Pour l'exégèse de Job 19,25-29,' *Zeitschrift für die Alttestamentliche Wissenschaft*, XXVI (1906), 143-46.

Budde, Karl. 'Job 24:12,' *Theologische Literatur-Zeitung*, (January, 1891), 3-28.

Cheyne, Thomas K. 'Job (Book), *Encyclopaedia Biblica*. Edited by T. K. Cheyne and J. S. Black. Vol. II, 1901.

Tieu, L. 'Le texte de Job du Codex Alexandrinus-ses principaux témoins,' *Le Muséon*, XIII (1912), 223-74.

----------. 'Nouveaux Fragments préhexaplaires du livre de Job en copte sahidique,' *Le Muséon*, XIII (1912), 147-85.

Donovan, W. N. 'Note on the LXX of Job 19:25-27,' *Journal of Biblical Literature*, LIV (1935), xii.

Draguet, Rene. 'Un commentair grec arien sur Job,' *Revue d'Histoire Ecclésiastique*, XX(1924), 38-66.

Driver, G. R. 'Problems in Job,' *American Journal of Semitic Languages and Literatures*, LII (April, 1936), 160-70.

Erman, Adolf. 'Das Verhältniss des Aegyptischen zu den semitischen Sprachen,' *Zeitschrift der Deutschen Morgenländischen Gesellschaft*. XLVI (1892), 93-129.

Flashar, Martin. 'Exegetische Studien zum Septuagintapsalter,' *Zeitschrift für die Alttestamentliche Wissenschaft*, XXXII (1912), 81-116; 161-89; 241-68.

Foster, Frank H. 'Is the Book of Job a Translation from an Arabic Original?,' *American Journal of Semitic Languages and Literatures*, XLIX (1932), 21-25.

Frankel, Z. 'Zur Frage über das Verhältniss des alexandrinischen und palästinischen Judenthums, namentlich in exegetischer Beziehung,' *Zeitschrift der Deutschen-Morgenländischen Gesellschaft*, IV (1850), 102-9.

Freudenthal, J. 'Are there Traces of Greek Philosophy in the LXX?,' *Jewish Quarterly Review*, II (1890), 205-22.

Fuchs, Hugo. 'Septuagint,' *The Universal Jewish Encyclopedia*. Edited by Isaac Landman. Vol. X, 1943.

Fullerton, K. 'Double Entendre in the First Speech of Eliphaz,' *Journal of Biblical Literature*, XLIX (1930), 320-74.

Gehman, Henry S. 'Job II,' *The Westminster Dictionary of the Bible*. Philadelphia: The Westminster Press, 1944.

------------. 'Versions,' *ibid*.

------------. 'The Theological Approach of the Greek Translator of Job 1-15,' *Journal of Biblical Literature*, LXVIII (September, 1949), 231-40.

------------. 'Exegetical Methods Employed by the Greek Translator of I Samuel,' *Journal of the American Oriental Society*, LXX (1950), 292-296.

------------. 'The Hebraic Character of Septuagint Greek,' *Vetus Testamentum*, I (1951), 81-90.

Gordis, Robert. 'Quotations as a Literary Usage in Biblical, Oriental, and Rabbinic Literature,' *Hebrew Union College Annual*, XXII (1949), 157-219.

Gray, G. Buchanan. 'The Additions in the Ancient Greek Version of Job,' *The Expositor*, June, 1920, 422-38.

Hontheim, J. 'Bemerkungen zu Iob 6-7,' *Zeitschrift für Katholische Theologie*, XXXIII (1899), 167-74.

------------. 'Das Buch Hiob als Strophisches Kunstwerk Nachgewiesen übersetzt und erklart,' *Biblische Studien*, IX (1904), Part III.

Irwin, William A. 'Poetic Structure in the Dialogue of Job,' *Journal of Near Eastern Studies*, V (January, 1946), 26-39.

Jeffrey, James. 'The NT and LXX compared with special reference to the Book of Job,' *The Expository Times*, XXXVI (1924), 70-73.

Jouon, Paul. 'Notes philologiques sur le texte hébreu de Job,' *Biblica*, XI (1939), 322-24.

Kennett, E. E. 'Job 28,' *The Expository Times*, XXXIII (1921-2), 426.

Landersdorfer, Simon. 'Eine babylonische Quelle fur das Buch Job?,' *Biblische Studien*, XVI (1911), Part II.

Ley, Julius. 'Charakteristik der drei Freunde Hiobs und der Wandlungen in Hiobs religiösen Anmerkungen,' *Theologische Studien und Kritiken*, LXXIII, 3 (1900), 331-63.

Liebermann, B.B. 'Job 17:11,' *The Expository Times*, XXXIV (1922-23), 330.

Liebreich, Leon. 'Notes on the Greek Version of Symmachus,' *Journal of Biblical Literature*, LXIII (1944), 397-403.

Lods, Adolphe. 'Recherches récentes sur le livre de Job,' *Revue d'Histoire et de Philosophie Religieuses*, XIV (1934), 501-33.

Lohr, M. 'Die Drei Bildad-Reden im Buch Hiob s. Budde-Festschrift 107-112,' *Zeitschrift für die Alttestamentliche Wissenschaft*, XXXVIII (1919-29), 177.

Martin, A. D. 'The Book of Job,' *The Expository Times*, XXVI, 2 (1914), 75-81.

Mowinckel, Sigmund. 'Hiobs gō'ēl und Zeuge im Himmel,' *Beihefte zür Zeitschrift für die Alttestamentliche Wissenschaft*, XLI (1925), 207-12.

Muller, K. 'Die Auslegung des Theodiceeproblems im Buche Hiob,' *Theologische Blätter*, I (1922), 73-79.

Nau, Francois. 'Etude sur Job XXXIX, 13 et sur les oiseaux fabuleux qui peuvent s'y rattacher,' *Journal Asiatique*, CCXV, 2 (1929), 193-236.

Nestle, Eberhard. 'David in the Book of Job,' *The Expository Times*, XXII, 2 (1910), 90.

Nichols, Helen H. 'The Composition of the Elihu Speeches,' *American Journal of Semitic Languages and Literatures*, XXVII (1911), 97-186.

Orlinsky, Harry M. ''Αποβαίνω and ἐπιβαίνω in the LXX of Job,' *Journal of Biblical Literature*, LVI (1937), 361-67.

------------. 'Job 5;8 -- A Problem in Greek-Hebrew Methodology,' *Jewish Quarterly Review*, XXV (1935), 271-78.

------------. 'Some Corruptions in the Greek Text of Job,' *Jewish Quarterly Review*, XXVI (1935-6), 133-45.

------------. 'The Hebrew and Greek Texts of Job 14:12,' *Jewish Quarterly Re-*

view, XXVIII (1937-8), 63-64.

Peake, Arthur S. 'Job 5:23,' *The Expository Times*, XXXIV (1922-23), 42-43.

Peters, N. 'Textkritisches zu Job,' *Theologische Quartalschrift*, LXXXIII (1901), 208-18; 389-96.

Posselt, Wenzel. 'Der Verfasser der Elihureden (Job Kap. 32-37),' *Biblische Studien*, XIV (1909), Part III.

Redpath, N. A. 'Mythological Terms in the LXX,' *American Journal of Theology*, IX (January, 1905), 34-45.

Reider, Joseph. 'שׂדד in Job 7,4,' *Journal of Biblical Literature*, XXXIX (1920), 60-65.

Shipley, A. E., and Cook. S. A. 'Jackal,' *Encyclopaedia Biblica*. Edited by T. K. Cheyne and J. S. Black. Vol II, 1901.

Speer, Julius. 'Zur Exegese von Hiob 19:25-27,' *Zeitschrift für die Alttestamentliche Wissenschaft*, XXV (1905), 47-140.

Sperber, A . 'Der Alphabet der Septuaginta-Vorlage,' *Orientalische Literatur-Zeitung*, XXXII (1929), 533-39.

Stummer, F. 'Beitrage zu dem Problem *Hieronymus und die Targumim*,' *Biblica*, XVIII (1937), 174-81.

Sutcliffe, E. F. 'Notes on Job, Textual and Exegetical,' *Biblica*, XXX (1949), 66-90.

Terrien, S. L. 'The Babylonian Dialogue on Theodicy and the Book of Job,' *Journal of Biblical Literature*, LXIII (1944), vi.

The Universal Jewish Encyclopedia. Vol. I. Article, 'Aristeas.'

Vaccari, A. 'Scripsitne Beda commentarium in Iob?,' *Biblica*, V (1924), 369-73.

Vetter, Paul. 'Die Metrik des Buches Job,' *Biblische Studien*, II (1897), Part IV.

Walde, B. 'Die Esdrasbucher der Septuaginta,' *Biblische Studien*, XVIII (1913), Part IV.

Waterman, Leroy. 'Note on Job 28:4,' *Journal of Biblical Literature*, LXXI (1952), 167-70.

Wevers, John W. 'Principles of Interpretation Guiding the Fourth Translator of the Book of the Kingdoms,' *Catholic Biblical Quarterly*, XIV (January, 1952), 40-56.

Wolff, M. 'Analekten,' *Zeitschrift der Deutschen Morgenländischen Gesellschaft*, LIV (1900), 8-16.

Wolk, S. J. B. 'Job,' *The Universal Jewish Encyclopedia.* Edited by Isaac Landmann. Vol. VI, 1942.

Zimmermann, F. 'Supplementary Observations on Job 40:2,' *American Journal of Semitic Languages and Literatures,* LI (October, 1934), 46-47.

Zolli, F. 'Note di Lessicografia Biblica,' *Biblica,* XXXVII (1946), 127-28.

Zorell,Franz. 'Der Gottesname *Šaddai* in den alten Uebersetzungen,' *Biblica,* VIII (1927), 215-19.

107

ADDENDA ET CORRIGENDA

Page 23, line 4: ὁμουμαδόν error for ὁμοθυμαδόν.

-------, footnote 1: *Reliquous* error for *Reliquos*.

Pages 39ff.: Cf., an interpretation of Job 19:25 given by Ralph Marcus in the
 Review of Religion (November, 1949), 5-29, 'Job and God': 'And as
 for me, would that I might know my vindicator in my lifetime!'.

Page 48, line 7: '. . . even thou stated negatively . . .', thou error for though.

Page 63, line 13: 'afflications' error for 'afflictions'.

Page 74, line 33: זבובית error for וזבובית.

Page 81, line 26: The meaning of the infinitive ברוח in M 27:22b could perhaps
 better be rendered in context as 'He *certainly* (*surely, i.e., hastily*)
 fleeth away from his (God's) hand.'

Page 194: Cf., a relevant article of Ralph Marcus's, 'Jewish and Greek Elements in
 the LXX,' Louis Ginzberg Jubilee Volume (New York, 1945), i, 227-246.

www.ingramcontent.com/pod-product-compliance
Lightning Source LLC
Chambersburg PA
CBHW020917090426
42736CB00008B/676